CREATING YOUR OWN SHARPER IMAGE®

Richard Thalheimer
helps you grow and manage your business and your life.

By Richard Thalheimer

Table of Contents

Table of Contents

Chapter 1

An Overview

I'm Richard Thalheimer, founder of The Sharper Image. Since I started the company almost 30 years ago I've loved being an entrepreneur, seeing how a business grows and what the ingredients are. That's why I want to share some ideas with you to help you grow your business, and to make your business reflect your image and your values. Not difficult ideas particularly, but common-sense ideas that you can use every day in almost every business endeavor.

If you're an entrepreneur like me, the problems and solutions suggested in this book are the types of situations that all of us deal with. There are common challenges in every business, regardless of its particular type. Sometimes we develop our own solutions on the spot, and over the years we learn what works best for us. You've probably already run into problems relating to hiring, supervising, marketing, technology, cash flow, and all the many challenges that come up every day, every week and every month.

Those are the kinds of ideas I'll discuss in this book. Some of these ideas apply to your situation more than others, and you'll need to modify some of the advice to fit your particular business. Hopefully the principles will be the same and it will have some real usefulness. And remember, if you have a different point of view or disagree, that's what it's all about.

You wouldn't be in business for yourself or trying to carve out your own unique career except for the fact that you do have independent ideas and you are a confident thinker. Entrepreneurs often see things differently, and that's fine. Take what you want, discard the rest. Surely you'll find a few good ideas here to help you. This is really just food for thought, so enjoy yourself.

A very brief history.

Let me just cover a little bit of the history of The Sharper Image. It started about 30 years ago when I got out of college and decided I wanted to come to San Francisco and start a business. This was 1971. I had grown up in Little Rock, Arkansas, and after getting out of college in New Haven, Connecticut, I went back to Little Rock briefly then packed up my Volkswagen and headed out to San Francisco, California. I didn't know exactly what I wanted to do, but I had spent a summer selling office supplies, copier paper and toner, so I knew how to knock on doors in the financial district and I knew how to get a wholesale source for these supplies.

So there I was on Route 66 headed across the southwest, driving into San Francisco at eight o'clock in the morning. Fortunately I headed to one of the nicest areas in the city where I found a "for rent" sign on a telephone pole right there in Pacific Heights, one of the choice neighborhoods. I signed the apartment lease that afternoon, unpacked my few things, and the next morning I headed down to the financial district to start knocking on doors.

So there I am. I'm selling paper and toner, I'm introducing myself to office purchasing managers, I'm learning how to sell directly. I had a little business, making deliveries in the morning, calling on offices in the afternoon and typing invoices at night on my coffee table. And I was thinking, I want to have a much bigger business someday. Why don't I go to law school and learn about contracts and business?

Once I began attending law school the next year, I realized I didn't have as much time to knock on doors and call my customers directly for my office supply business, so I decided to send out mail order fliers and circulars. Wouldn't you know it; that worked pretty darn well.

Then I thought, this is interesting, why don't I mail it someplace else, mail it outside of San Francisco. I mean, I've never met these people, but try it, what the heck? And amazingly, it worked. I'm mailing out these letters and fliers,

3

the orders are coming in, I'm shipping and it's working without me ever calling on anyone in person. And I'm thinking, wow, this mail order is so exciting. You create an ad, and once you get the formula right you can mail it out to thousands of people or maybe even millions.

Okay, so this is going along pretty well. Then an interesting thing happens. I'm in this running club and everybody wants to get one of the new chronographs, those waterproof digital wristwatch stopwatches that you wear on your wrist, but they're expensive, like $300, but they're very useful. They compute time, they're waterproof and they can take the sweat. Before you know it (it must have been fate) someone told me to go to the consumer electronics show in Las Vegas and look around. So I did, and I find an importer who's come up with the same idea as the $300 Seiko chronograph, but I can afford to sell it for $70. I'm thinking, this is incredible, what a bargain.

I'd been reading *Runner's World* magazine, I know that runners want this watch, so I'm thinking, why don't I do a full-page ad in *Runner's World* magazine for this watch? I already know how to sell things. I've been doing it with the office supply business. So I write the ad myself. It was a fun ad, and before I knew it thousands of orders were coming in.

Before I could take a breath a year had gone by, I was 27 years old, I had made almost a million dollars selling this one watch, and I thought this is really exciting. By that time I had finished law school and I was practicing law a bit, but I thought, selling is much more exciting than practicing law. I'm going to expand this to lots of other magazines. So I did. Then I thought, why don't I find another product? I introduced the first cordless telephone and that was very successful. Remember back a long time ago when we had never heard of a cordless telephone? It's hard to remember that long ago. Then along came the first car radar detector, the first home answering machine and a host of other products.

All the ads did pretty well. Some did better than others, but they all did well enough. So then I thought, why don't I try a color catalog grouping these products together? I had built up a list at that point of different customers and I knew I could find a few more new products, so in 1979 the first catalog went out.

At that time I put every penny I had into that catalog mailing and if it hadn't been successful I probably would have gone out of business right then, but I knew my market, and I knew my products. I made a calculated estimate that there was no way I would really lose any money, so I had the odds in my favor as I sent out that catalog, and it worked all right. Before I knew it, people were coming up to the office trying to buy these products, so in 1981 I said, why don't we open a store so these people have someplace to shop? Even though the store was in a quiet neighborhood in downtown San Francisco it did great right from the beginning.

Now fast-forward about 27 years later, and today there's about 200 Sharper Image stores, the business is approaching a billion dollars a year, we have a wonderful hundred-million-dollar-plus Internet business, a terrific catalog and there have been so many ups and downs it's like a roller coaster ride at Six Flags. Fortunately during the last decade everything has gotten better because we've learned what works and what doesn't, and that's what I want to share with you, what has worked and what I've learned from this school of hard knocks. There's a joke that Mother Nature gives the experience before she gives the lesson. That's certainly been my experience. Lots of things have happened and I wish I had known the lesson before I got the experience. But I've learned a lot, and that's what we're sharing in this book.

What is The Sharper Image today?

Many of you know it, some of you may not, so quickly, here's the strategy of The Sharper Image: To share the fun of discovering products that make life easier and more enjoyable.

When we first started, we sold products for male executives, boy's toys, and as the years went by it evolved to become a different type of business model. Instead of selling suits of armor or a James Bond crossbow or a custom Harley-Davidson, more and more our slogan became Sharper Image for Everyone, because today we sell a range of products that are often fun but also very useful.

Whether it's the nose and ear hair trimmer, or an air purifier, or a hair dryer for women that conditions the hair while it dries, or a small piece of exercise equipment, or the world's first automatic eyeglass cleaner, or one of our music products that has a sound soother environment library built in, our products today are so useful and cover such a broad demographic that we can honestly say it is Sharper Image for Everyone. Price points range from 10 dollars to several thousand, but typically a product might only be $20, $30, $40 or $50.

Because our product mix has shifted from men's products to products that appeal equally to men and women, because our price points are much broader than they were 10 or 20 years ago, because the products are useful and functional as well as fun, we can now open up stores in almost any city, any suburb, any location. Our catalog, as well as our Internet site, appeals to a much broader audience. This has enabled us to grow from a humble beginning to an almost billion-dollar business today and allowed us to achieve terrific sales gains over the past few years.

The Sharper Image that you may have seen 10 or 20 years ago isn't the Sharper Image you see today. All businesses continue to evolve and change. The Sharper Image certainly has. It seems we've reinvented ourselves a number of times, over and over, to keep the business alive and growing. I probably had that in mind when I came up with the name for The Sharper Image. I wanted something that would let it expand into new areas and not confine it to any one thing. So let's talk about names.

What's in a name?

When I went to the San Francisco financial district to start knocking on doors I needed a name for my new business. It's not difficult to make up business cards and stationery, but it is difficult to come up with a good name. Because the law usually requires you to register your business, and because it is more difficult to register a fictitious name, one that's not the same as your legal name, I chose to go the easy route. I used my own name for the business, Thalheimer Paper Systems. That made it easier to get registered with the City of San Francisco. You'll notice, however, this does not exactly roll off the tongue.

I love business names that are catchy, easy to read and pronounce. Some of my personal favorites are Microsoft, Gap, Land Rover, Starbucks, Intel, Lexus, Tiffany, IBM, Domino's Pizza and Hummer. They're easy to spell and remember, they sound good when you pronounce them.

Names that are hard to pronounce and don't roll off the tongue make the customer, or your potential customer, work a lot harder. Sometimes it causes difficulty in spelling it out for the Internet. For example, who can spell or easily pronounce Hammacher Schlemmer, the famous catalog company? That's a hard one to put in an Internet navigation bar. Does it have a hyphen? Are there four Ms or just three in Hammacher Schlemmer? We've all learned to spell Gucci, but I can still barely spell or pronounce Yves Saint Laurent or Altria or Hyundai. They're just not easy to spell or remember. A name that's easy to remember and pronounce is a great asset to any start-up business.

I knew the name Thalheimer Paper Systems had to go eventually. I kept thinking of names and one day "The Sharper Image" popped into my mind. I wanted a name that would let me sell the imaging and copier supplies that I already had, but I also thought this would let me sell just about anything someday. I'll never forget a few years later when I hired my first creative director. He asked if I would consider changing the name. He thought it was too long and difficult for magazine ads. By then I really liked the name and I wouldn't consider changing it. Now, he was a brilliant creative director and helped me so much, but I knew my customers and my image.

From that I learned it's good to trust your own instincts, sometimes even in the face of contradictory advice from a professional who often knows a lot more than you do. Just realize it's your business and you know it best. I wasn't about to change the name. So I kept the name and now years later it still works extremely well.

Over the years The Sharper Image has sold everything imaginable: a two-person submarine; customized Harley-Davidson motorcycles; a knight's suit of armor; autographed sheet music from the Beatles; original art from Peter Max; restored collectible cars; luxury condominiums; and many really interesting and unique items. With a name like The Sharper Image we can sell anything and everything.

For your endeavor you may prefer a name that's more specific and tells people exactly what you're doing. For example, Hans' German Motors or Home Computer Solutions or Bruno's Little Italy might work better if you want to communicate a purpose or a service and still have some flair. But you can still be original. Instead of Hans' German Motors, maybe Precision German Motors or

Efficient Home Computer Solutions, for a better twist on the same idea. Get the benefit right up there in the headline.

Your business name is a great headline and calling card. You want it to do as much as it can. Of course you want to be proud of the name of your business. You're going to sell it to others, ask them to give you business and be known by this name for a long time. Put a lot of thought into it and it will serve you well.

Pursue what you love.

Have you noticed how some people work their entire life so they can eventually retire and stop working, and others seem to want to work forever, retiring only when they're finally forced to stop because of health issues or company policy? Having a fulfilling occupation that you love is probably the single biggest predictor of success. It is so much more fun to wake up in the morning with a genuine desire to go to work, and we do so much better at our work with this attitude. It's not easy for everyone to find the work they love, but it is much easier to do good work if you love what you do. Your challenge is to find an area that stimulates and excites you.

Last night I was watching Suze Orman, the financial adviser, on television. Wow. She clearly enjoys giving financial advice and doing her television show and writing financial books. You see the same love of performing on "The Tonight Show with Jay Leno" or "Late Night with David Letterman"; they really enjoy doing it. That's the way I've always felt about my job. I love buying products or thinking up new product ideas or taking an existing product and figuring out how to make it better. It's a very creative and satisfying process that fulfills me.

Sometimes you already have a good product or service, maybe even an excellent one, and the challenge is to figure out how to market it. I discovered a long time ago that having a great product is one thing; selling it is another. It doesn't do any good to have the best idea in the world if you can't sell it.

Making money is what people often say they want to do, but that's not what a career or a business is really about. Making money doing something you love is so much better. Sometimes making money doing something you love is not as important as just doing something you love, because that's what allows you to do it night and day for a long time, with that same feeling of excitement when you wake up in the morning to take on another day.

It can take years to build your success, even decades. If you're going to work at something for 10 or 20 years, you want to love doing it. It's always struck me as unusual that people fall into a career choice in college, then eventually go to graduate school, and then get a job without ever really deciding whether or not they love what they do. Of course this varies tremendously from person to person. Some do choose early on what they want to do and they love it their entire lifetime. But others are different and perhaps work hard because they need the income to support a family or build security, but they really don't enjoy what they do.

I always felt that I needed and wanted to be in a business of my own where I was the boss, though it wasn't apparent to me at a young age exactly what that business would be. From my personal experience it doesn't seem so important to know at a young age exactly what you want to do. It may work better for some of us to discover it later. What is important is to do something you can throw yourself into without reservation.

One of my personal favorite success stories is Colonel Harland Sanders. He's the founder of a chain of fast food restaurants called Kentucky Fried Chicken, now called KFC. Colonel Sanders was living and sleeping in his car when finally in his 60s he began to build his hugely successful enterprise. After a lifetime of struggle he achieved remarkable results with his pioneering national fast food franchise. It shows that anyone can build a successful business, even starting at an age that most of us think of as retirement rather than career building. Most importantly, he had a passion, he loved what he did and he didn't stop until he made it a success.

Your business should be as original as you are.

America has become a sophisticated marketplace and the Internet makes it easy to compare prices on the make and model of every product. If you can be distinctive in the marketplace and not be price-shopped for the same items elsewhere, you've got a big advantage. So many businesses are alike; yours should be different. If your business is unique it's less vulnerable to being copied or knocked off by a bigger competitor.

Larger, more established players have copied lots of start-ups. In 1980, when The Sharper Image was really getting going, there were literally a dozen knock-off catalogs trying to copy what we were doing. They looked a lot like us.

There were also stores in the shopping malls that copied the look and feel of our stores. One year the Macy's department store here in San Francisco even put in an entire floor that looked exactly like you were in The Sharper Image. Even the fixtures were copied and the products were the same. I was so discouraged by that.

About 1990 I realized we really had a problem. If we were going to survive and grow and prosper we had to have unique products. We had unique products when we started in the '80s. The problem was we were so successful that by the '90s everyone was copying and buying the same items, and they could copy the look of the catalog and the look of the stores. So the challenge was very clear. We had to reinvent ourselves and come up with a way to have unique products and unique packaging that no one else had.

I decided the only way to survive and prosper and to get out of this dilemma was to make — that is, manufacture — our own products. We had to come up with ideas from scratch, design the product, create the machine press tools, get the patents, make the electronic circuits and create the packaging. This was the way to be different and unique. It's also one of the most difficult approaches.

It takes a fair amount of distribution to justify manufacturing a product. Back then we were barely able to sell a production run of 3,000 units, so we begged a manufacturer to take an order that small. In other words, we designed the whole thing but we had to get some contract manufacturing plant to actually put it together.

To amortize the initial development cost over just 3,000 pieces was expensive. If there was a $50,000 or $60,000 upfront design expense, for 3,000 pieces that would come to almost $20 a piece just for the initial tooling. So the numbers wouldn't work very well unless we could eventually get to the point where we could sell 25,000 or 50,000 pieces of something; then the upfront investment would only be about a dollar each — a much more reasonable amount.

We made our first couple of products in 1993. One was the motorized tie rack that spins neckties around in your closet when you press the button, and the other was a key ring that featured a special way to organize and remove your keys. Fortunately they each sold better than we expected and eventually surpassed the 50,000-unit goal. Since then we've invented and made over 200 different products, making our business different from all the competitors that try to copy us.

Now, in 2004, approximately 80% of all our sales are unique products. Forty percent of everything we sell is invented by us and manufactured by us; another 40% is made up of products that we exclusively distribute and that have our packaging and our branding.

In other words, 80% of all our revenues today are earned by exclusive Sharper Image products — in our boxes, our brand, our packaging. We've accomplished the goal of creating unique, exclusive products and created a business that's quite distinctive from others. Two decades of building a solid culture of product creation makes it virtually impossible for a competitor to compete with us in our particular retail area.

This idea will work for you, too. No matter what your business is, you want it to be unique. All the advantages of uniqueness then work for you. It's easier to maintain your pricing, it's easier to hold onto your customers, it's easier to build long-term loyalty if your business has a special and original quality.

The special characteristics of your business can be made up of many parts. They can start with the name, the logo, the graphics. You might have a slogan that's unique to you or some visual clue. It might be unique music or visuals, if you do television or radio ads; and if that's the case, make it short, make it catchy and use it consistently.

Your products, if you're in the product manufacturing business, can be unique, or perhaps modified slightly in feature or color or appearance to be distinct from your competition. Your physical place of business might look special, or the employees may display something unique in their clothing or accessories. Whatever you chose to do and whatever area you're in, don't underestimate the importance of doing something original.

Success is 1% inspiration and 99% perspiration.

Thomas Edison was truly a great inventor, having created the first coated fiber electric light bulb, among many other brilliant inventions. Yet even such a brilliant guy as Mr. Edison said in his view success is 1% inspiration and 99% perspiration, meaning the effort and the follow-through is more important than the original idea.

That's been my experience as well. It's interesting how many times over the years I've met people and they've said to me, "Oh, you know, I had an idea to start a business like The Sharper Image. I should have followed up on it." Or maybe they said, "You know, I had this great product idea for so many years and I could have been rich if I'd gotten it to market." When I hear this I inwardly shrug and think to myself, they don't realize having a good idea is only the beginning.

Most of the variables leading to success are not the ideas, not the wishes, not the dreams, but being committed to making it happen. The actual work of creating success is a lot harder than the idea. This is the point where you need to just get started and keep moving in a positive direction. Sometimes it's so hard to move forward each day, but that's exactly what I used to do. Every day I'd ask myself, What have I done today not just to maintain what

I already have, but to actually move things forward into a new and bigger future?

So every day you have to do something, no matter how small, to make things move forward. It's easy to make excuses why today is not the day to get something done, but you have to overcome that temptation if you want to be more successful tomorrow than you are today. It's difficult to maintain this attitude month after month, year after year, but you can do it and you will. That's just part of being an entrepreneur.

Start small and finish big.

If you've always dreamed of starting out as one of those big, well-financed, money-heavy venture capital start-ups, then you're in the wrong place reading this book. I personally started out with a small step approach to building a business. Building up The Sharper Image one brick at a time was admittedly a very slow process, and it hasn't grown as quickly as some other businesses. On the other hand, it is a lot more solid because the foundation was slowly and carefully created over many years. Some companies that started fast also ended fast.

How small a step is too small to start? That's a good question. I've noticed that the most difficult thing about starting any new project is getting it off the ground. For me it's worked well to break down every objective, every goal into smaller and smaller steps until the first step is one that I can actually take and accomplish.

Remember the Bill Murray movie *What About Bob?* In this movie the character Bob is a neurotic patient who tries to follow the advice of his psychiatrist, played by Richard Dreyfuss. When he first comes in for therapy he's too frightened and anxious to accomplish anything on his own. Eventually he learns the successful technique of taking baby steps.

That's my approach, too. Sometimes that first step may be just making a phone call and asking about the availability of a product or a service. You may be fascinated to learn that what you're looking for isn't available and perhaps you should be offering it, or perhaps the prices are much higher or lower than you expected, which might give you an opportunity. Or perhaps the customer relations for that product area are terrible, again, giving you a chance to start something better. It is so inexpensive to make phone calls, to ask questions, to inquire; it takes nothing but your time. From those questions you'll discover the steps you want to take, and once you figure out the first step, then you'll probably see the second step, and so on.

Eventually you want to reach a goal. You want those baby steps to be leading somewhere — your vision of success. This analogy works in many situations. You may have run a marathon in your lifetime or known someone who did. If so, you probably know that a great technique for running long races is to start somewhat slowly and speed up throughout the race. The worst thing you can do is to sprint out of the start, then fade, then limp along and barely make it to the end. What you want is to start off at a slow, comfortable pace and accelerate throughout the race. Business and life are the same way. Ideally we want to start slow and finish strong.

Entrepreneurs are always optimists.

In case you didn't already know this, they are. Entrepreneurs are always optimists. That's because there's so much negative energy and so much adversity that entrepreneurs run into when they first start out, that if they weren't optimists they would get too depressed. What's an optimist? Probably a good definition is someone who sees the glass half full, or even completely full, rather than half empty. I'm always looking at that half full glass and thinking, Wow, we could take this half full glass and make it really full. Here's how to do it. Others will of course give you a hard time, and they will always tell you the reasons why something won't work. This never fails to amaze me. People, especially those with backgrounds in finance or accounting, are likely to discourage you and tell you why it can't be done.

When I decided that we should begin designing, creating and manufacturing our own products, so many people told me that was a prescription for disaster, and of course they'd feel that way. Who would think that a retailer could start creating and manufacturing his own products? And yet ten years later it turned out to be the key to our success. Now our products are different from everyone else's, they have better margins and they make The Sharper Image unique, so it worked out perfectly. But there were so many objections that if I had listened to them all we would have never done it.

One of my favorite sayings is, "If all objections must be overcome, nothing will ever be accomplished." Isn't that the truth? Waiting until all the objections are overcome will definitely prevent any project from being launched or completed.

Now, don't get me wrong here. There are plenty of people who fail because they work in the wrong order. They go "ready, fire, aim." That's probably not going to be a successful approach either. You need to have a plan and you need to carry out the plan accurately, but that's different from planning so long and so thoroughly that nothing ever gets started, much less ever gets finished.

I'll never forget the first MBA (Master of Business Administration) that worked with me. This was a fellow from Stanford and he had a terrible time getting started on any project. Instead, we would discuss the project, then he would go to his office, pull out his legal pad and start analyzing and writing and strategizing. I'd drop by a day or two later and he'd still be writing on this legal pad. And I thought to myself, Oh gosh, you've got to get started. We would never start a project, we would never initiate the first step, there was no baby step; there was just writing on a legal pad. I thought, this is so the opposite of the way I am.

We parted ways after about a month. You can't just keep doodling forever. You've got to take action. I call it a sense of urgency. My sense of urgency is much higher than most people's. It's the reason I get things done.

I like to get started with however small a step is necessary, and I see that same trait in successful managers. Their sense of urgency to get things done is so important to the overall result. When you combine the optimistic view that says things can be done with the sense of urgency to take a step today to make things happen, you've got a powerful combination of factors carrying you toward your goal.

Bathtub visions.

When I started my first business, the one selling office supplies door to door, I often wondered where it might lead someday and how I would get there. One technique worked well for me. It may not be the one for you, but I'm sure you'll develop your own version of it. When I first started out I was renting a great apartment that didn't have a shower, oddly enough, but it had a great bathtub. So I would take long baths after a hard day of work, and while sitting in the hot water I would let my mind wander and I would think about two things: One, where was I in my business, and two, where did I want to be a year down the road or five years or 10 years?

I realized where I was in the present. I was a door-to-door salesman knocking on doors in the financial district of San Francisco selling copier paper, and 10 or 20 years down the road I wanted to have a large company selling a variety of products all over the country. So I know where I am, I know where I want to be; how do I get from here to there?

You could call it daydreaming, letting one's visions float, but that's the only way to do this. I really believe that only when you visualize your dreams can you actually achieve them. Visions are just that; they're fantasies, but you have to have the fantasy and the vision of what you eventually want if you're to have any hope of actually getting there. Putting it another way, if you don't fantasize or have visions, you're a lot less likely to ever realize those dreams. And don't let anyone discourage you from visualizing a terrific success down the road. Your fantasies will more likely become realities once you know what they are and start working on those steps to get there.

By the way, after that bathtub apartment, I moved, and I really haven't had a great bathtub since, but I have found that long, solitary walks are a great substitute — probably better because you get some exercise while you're daydreaming. Long bike rides work well, especially if you don't like your bike saddle; you can fantasize about business instead. Whatever gives you time to reflect, to analyze and to daydream is an important part of your future planning, so don't ever think that daydreaming is a waste of time. That is certainly not true. Visualizing your fantasies is one of the most meaningful steps toward reaching your goals.

Have you set your sights too low?

This is the opposite from setting your sights too high. When I first started my business my goals evolved from month to month and year to year. I fantasized about having a really large company someday, but I was also conscious that my immediate-term goals were simply to double the size of the business during the coming year. So I devised some specific steps: how to get from here to there, how I was going to reach that goal of doubling it. For example, I decided I would spend twice as much because I would mail out twice as many catalogs, and that way I would double the revenues.

On one hand I had specific short- and intermediate-term goals. On the other hand, even if they were met and they were successful, it was still a limited goal. Some years my goals weren't so ambitious. Perhaps one year my goal would be to keep the business at the same level and not let the volume drop, or maybe it would be to grow it by 20%.

The point I'm making is that you need to set goals that are ambitious enough so if they are met, you're moving along at a growth pace that's taking you where you want to be. You don't want to work hard for 20 years and end up with a successful small business that can't support your needs.

Ask yourself, even if I am successful in my goal, where does that really put me in five or 10 years? Will it be enough, or is it really a lower level of income and success than I need to live? It's a balancing act. You want to set achievable goals; you don't want them to be so high you can't reach them, but on the other hand you want to set them high enough so that when these goals are reached you're where you want to be.

Sometimes that requires us to switch careers altogether. It might be that the first profession you entered was something that turned out not to be satisfying to you, that you didn't love doing. Perhaps you thought you would enjoy the work and discovered you didn't, or perhaps down the road to accomplishment you realize your chosen field isn't going to provide the level of income you need. Maybe it's that the company you're working for isn't recognizing your talents and you need to change jobs, change careers or change companies.

For a variety of reasons people become dissatisfied and change positions or fields. This is part of the overall strategy of moving up and is perfectly normal. You should be constantly reevaluating your situation and asking yourself if you are pleased with the progress you're making. If not, start thinking about how to change it. Feeling this sort of dissatisfaction can really be a positive influence and a positive driver for you to reach your life goals. You want to be fully engaged and entirely satisfied with what you're doing and where it's taking you.

Chapter 2

How to Win Customers

The business greeting...or lack of it.

I don't want to overlook one of my favorite topics: how to greet people. It's the same whether you're selling on a sales floor, calling on an office manager or starring in a television news show or infomercial. It begins with real eye contact. Look directly at the other person or directly into the camera lens and never look away from that spot. Seriously, it looks shifty to have shifting eyes.

Give the person a warm smile and a greeting of hello in a tone of voice that says to the other person, I feel great, I'm a warm and likeable human being, and I'm happy to be here to greet you. I'm conveying an emotion of interest, warmth and enthusiasm. Does that seem a bit over the top? You can tone it down to your level, but trust me, most people will respond a lot more positively to someone who is warm and enthusiastic. It's hard to make a sale when the customer perceives you as aloof, cold or distant.

I've never tired of telling the story about walking into my suburban Porsche automobile dealership a few years ago. Although I had purchased two different Porsches from this dealer over a period of about 10 years, no one recognized me or greeted me that particular day. However, there was a salesperson supervising the floor whom I'd never seen before, sort of a gruff, crusty gentleman who was on duty that day, but he didn't get up from his desk or even acknowledge that I walked into the showroom. Here I am actually dressed in a coat and tie walking into a Porsche dealership and this person doesn't even acknowledge my presence. Instead, he shot me a cursory glance, didn't realize I was actually one of their most frequent customers, and dismissed me with a curt inquiry as to whether or not I needed help.

His unfriendly tone made me certain I didn't want any help from him, so I left the dealership and didn't return for about a year or so. I did tell the story quite a few times though, adding a little bit of bad word of mouth every time because I enjoyed telling the story. About a year later, I returned to the dealership and met a salesperson who had sold me a Porsche in the past. He was so warm and enthusiastic. What a difference! It totally turned me around and makes me want to buy from them again.

Sharper Image salespeople are asked to greet everyone with enthusiasm. Some do it better than others. Some perhaps are a little bit shy — they're not people persons. We really don't want to hire salespeople that are not outgoing, warm and enthusiastic, but sometimes it happens because we don't know until they get into the job. Unless they transition into real greeters with genuine warmth and personality, they won't accomplish the sales results they need, and they probably won't make it in the long term. That's just the way it is in sales. You must make the other person want to do business with you. Whether it's a restaurant or a brokerage firm, the customer wants to be wanted, and wants to be treated well. Recognize this even if you don't think of yourself or your business as sales. Everyone needs to convince others of the desirability of seeing him or her again in a professional context.

Whether you're talking with your doctor or lawyer or acupuncturist or house painter, you don't need to spend your hard-earned money on any of them when there are other choices. To a certain extent they're selling you on having confidence that they're the one you want to do business with.

Sometimes we don't realize we're in fact selling someone on wanting to do business with us, but believe me, we are. Business is really about relationships. We all want to be treated well in our relationships and business is no exception.

Customer relations in three easy steps.

One big advantage I have in business is that I'm secure enough to be able to say I messed up. That may sound easy to do, but a lot of people cannot admit they made a mistake. Has that happened to you? Have you ever started to complain to a store or a business about a problem, hoping they would just admit their mistake and you would appreciate it so much if they would just tell you how sorry they are that they screwed up? It's funny how this works. A lot of the time the person you're talking to gets defensive and has a difficult time accepting your criticism. So now you're frustrated and you're probably not going to want to do business with them again.

This happens all the time. The defensive store clerk or store manager blames it on something else: it's the computer's fault, or they didn't make the reservation or some other excuse. Why not use simple approaches to customer relations that work and make everyone happy and bring the customer back again?

Here is the easiest approach to customer relations ever, which takes the upset customer and turns the situation into a positive. This is what you or your business should do when confronted with an angry customer. First, admit you made a mistake and apologize sincerely for the problem. Repeating the customer's complaint is a good idea. It shows you heard what they said. Second, ask the customer what they'd like you to do to rectify the situation. After all, what the customer thinks they want is usually what they want. Giving them what *you* want is a common mistake. Try to incorporate elements of what they are asking for in your suggestion to them. And third, promptly take action to show the customer you are genuinely attempting to solve the problem, or at least improve the situation. And if at all possible, give the customer more than they expected from you or more than they asked for.

Now you're wondering, what about the situation where in reality it was the customer's mistake and not yours? Should you still apologize and try to make it right? Absolutely! Because the customer doesn't see it any other way. They wouldn't have brought it up unless they felt they had been wronged somehow.

It really is not about who's right or who's wrong anyway. It's about making the customer feel that you have a responsive business that's catering to him or her, right then, and on their terms. Give up the idea of straightening out the problem by convincing the customer that it's their mistake. It just doesn't work that way.

Besides, your mission is not to convince them that they're wrong. Your mission is to make them want to buy from your business again and again, and the surest way to do that is to make them understand your business is one that listens and responds to the customer. If in fact you positively cannot afford to give them what they want, and it really is not your fault in any way and they are totally wrong, then do a modification of this approach. Give total lip service to the apology, give total lip service to the customer, and describe your intention to make it right. Then make whatever offer you can make, describing it to them in the most positive terms possible. That's a pragmatic approach, and once in awhile that's what you have to do.

One of the sayings I like is that any business can take an order well, but only a great business can handle a problem well. Why not view every customer problem as an opportunity to show what a great business you have and to leave the customer feeling they want to give more business to you in the future? If you give the customer more than they expected they will spread great word of mouth about you, and they'll tell their friends, "I can't believe The Sharper Image did this for me," or gave me a new unit, or exchanged it so quickly, or whatever. They might say, "I went into The Sharper Image, I had this problem and they took care of it right away. Can you believe a business would treat you that well?" Now that's the positive word of mouth that you'd like to have circulating about your business, and it's worth so much more than it costs to create.

Selling techniques that really work.

Here are some simple selling techniques that every experienced professional person uses. If you know them, you'll recognize them. If you don't, these are wonderful, easy-to-learn techniques that really help you make sales and make a close.

Here's the situation: The sales rep has had a conversation with a prospective customer. It could be in a retail store, or a sales call, or a phone conversation, or any situation where there's been some conversation about a potential deal or purchase. Now the customer has stopped talking and the moment has arrived. The sales rep needs to do one thing that's very important. They need to ask a question that is deliberately designed to lead toward a close. Let me give you some examples. "Mr. Prospect, do you think you'd like to get the red one or the blue one?" That right there is one of the simplest closing techniques possible. You give the prospect a choice. Would you like to get the small or the medium? Do you prefer the leather or the Naugahyde? Let's look at some more examples.

"Ms. Purchasing Agent, do you want to set up the contract to get the automatic delivery with the discount that I mentioned?" or "Ms. Jones, do you want to me to start setting up an incentive program for your sales staff?" or "Mr. Thomas, how many machines do you want to order for your first shipment?" or "Mr. Chang, is that price attractive enough so that we can place an order today?" As you can see, each of these questions is one that requires a response from the perspective buyer, and every question is a header toward a close.

Having asked the question, don't forget to be quiet and let the other person answer. Sometimes a moment of silence is okay. Let the seconds tick by, don't say anything; let them respond first and listen carefully. If their answer is not an immediate offer to complete the transaction, be prepared to acknowledge their objection and ask the next question. "All right, that makes sense. How about if I call you in two weeks to see if you're ready to place an order then?" or "Mr. Chang, I'm disappointed the price still hasn't tempted you. Is it okay if I sharpen my pencil and call you in two days to see if it's possible to give you an even better price?" or "Ms. Jones, since you've said it's premature to set up the new incentive program now, would it be acceptable if I refine the presentation and come up with what might be an even more interesting program? I'd like to come back next week and show you both. How about Wednesday?"

Obviously, you're doing two things here. You've given them a chance to close and you're avoiding taking no for an answer. Instead, you're shifting toward a future opportunity to make the close. Most importantly, you're keeping the relationship alive and healthy. It's not ending; it's just momentarily postponed. There's a big difference. Someone who's really not used to selling will sometimes try to make the close, hear the no, leave and that's the end of it. But you don't want that to be the end. Successful salespeople intuitively know this and do it all the time. For those just starting, it takes a little bit more effort at first, but eventually it will become second nature. Attempt to close, don't take no for an answer, leave yourself an out, and make a commitment for a future conversation.

How long do you want to keep a customer?

Since we're talking about customers let's think about this question: how long do you want to keep a particular customer coming back to your business? Is it just long enough for them to complete this one purchase and this purchase only? That might work if you're selling your house to one person, one time, after 25 years of living there. You don't care if that person ever comes back; you won't be selling your house again. On the other hand, if you are running a fast food franchise like McDonalds, that approach doesn't work at all. You need that customer to come back lots of times, again and again, year after year.

That's certainly true of The Sharper Image. I want customers to come back at least once, maybe twice a year, and sometimes a lot more than that. And I want to keep the customer for many years to come. It's interesting how many customers have followed The Sharper Image, and continue to buy from us for 20 years or more. Partly they do this because we treat them so well. Some years we may have had several products they wanted, maybe fewer products another year. Regardless, those customers always appreciate the way they were treated, the courtesy, the respect, the return privilege, help with a repair, a refund or any other assistance that we offer.

As a result, there are very few past customers who aren't ready to come back to The Sharper Image and shop with us again. They're ready to come in and see what's new, to buy for themselves or to buy a gift, because we have a history with them. We've treated them well in the past, they've had great interactions with us and they're totally open to coming back.

Here's an interesting fact. When you work out the dollars and cents, it is so much less expensive to keep a customer you already have, than to spend the money to get a new customer. Some businesses overlook that. They're willing to lose a customer now and then, but they don't realize it will cost them five times as much to get a brand new one to replace the one they lost. There's a big up-front cost in converting a prospect or a non-customer to a customer.

It costs much less to accommodate a reasonable request, or an almost reasonable request, by the current customer rather than run the risk that they'll never shop with you again. Treat your customers like you want them to come back again and again for 20 or 40 years.

We practice that at The Sharper Image every single day. Don't forget, most customers think they're right. Your job is never to convince them they're wrong. Rather, receive and validate their dissatisfaction when they have a complaint and treat them like royalty all the time. Your job is to make them want to buy again and again and again.

Treat your suppliers like your customers.

Here's an argument that your vendors, that is, your suppliers, are just as important to your future as your customers. After all, they're the ones that provide the inventory and support services that keep your business going. Why shouldn't they be treated just like a customer? You really need to keep them happy. This is not an obvious concept for some people to understand. There's something that doesn't resonate right away about the assertion that vendors should be treated as well as customers.

Over the years I've observed our own buyers, our purchasing agents at The Sharper Image, sometimes treat vendors as if they're second class citizens. Occasionally a vendor may be in a compromised position: they're holding inventory or burdened with a necessary expense or inconvenience, and the buyer is unsympathetic because they may feel the seller is in a subservient role to the buyer.

To me that is just plain wrong. For one thing, word of mouth circulates among your supplier community. You want positive word of mouth, and you want dedicated loyalty from your suppliers. You want them to come to your aid when you need them.

I remember the terribly difficult recession of 1990 and how some of our major suppliers, even large ones like Sony or Panasonic, were cutting back on the credit available to us at The Sharper Image. We were actually doing fine, but they had gotten burned by some larger department stores, such as when Macy's declared bankruptcy, and they were afraid it might spread to other retailers like us. They weren't very loyal suppliers and they made our life a lot more difficult than it needed to be.

The medium-size and smaller suppliers, on the other hand, were so steadfast and loyal, they did everything they could to help us get through a difficult year. For example, at our request they looked through their costs, they passed along savings where possible, they even extended our credit terms during the Christmas holiday season so that normal 30-day terms were extended to 60 or 90 days instead. We got this just by asking. Realistically, the smaller vendors need you as much as you need them. This really helped us get by at a time of year when the extra inventory and the payment terms were critical.

It's interesting how many times over several decades I've received letters from suppliers telling me that somehow they were accidentally mistreated by one of our buyers. I'm not proud to say that, but it happened occasionally over the years. For example, being asked to cancel a purchase order at the last minute and absorb the costs, which can be devastating to a small manufacturer or supplier.

The problem is that the buyer honestly thinks he or she is doing a good job for The Sharper Image by being tough on the vendor. They're perhaps overlooking the big picture, however: we need our vendors to support us. Over the years I've tried my best to train our buyers otherwise, and I want to pass that same thought along to you. Understand, we don't want to take advantage of a vendor because we can. Rather, we want to treat them as customers, and continue to build solid relationships that we will cultivate and keep intact for many years.

You'll meet the same people coming down the ladder as you did climbing up.

Have you heard that before? The fact is, what goes around comes around, and people have long memories. In everything you do you create a reputation for yourself and your business. Remember, there's a certain likelihood that someone you step on, or anger, or take advantage of, is going to come back and cause you problems later in your career. You don't want them to carry a grudge against you or try to get even for the way you treated them 10 years ago.

This saying appears in many different cultures. I think there's a Chinese proverb that goes, "Don't muddy the puddles along the road. You may need to drink from the same puddles on your return trip." It makes the same point, which is that fair and even-handed treatment of your colleagues creates a better reputation for you in your community and in the business network where headhunters and recruiters call for references. Of course they call all the places where you've worked in the past.

I actually believe in karma. Your good karma helps you throughout your career, and bad karma will hurt you eventually. Stay positive. There's no good reason to have enemies out there. You need all the support and all the positive word of mouth you can get. Even when people don't get along with me I try to part ways with them on good terms. At The Sharper Image this even leads to good-bye parties and nice send-offs for people who are leaving.

They may be leaving The Sharper Image to take another job, but we still often throw a party for them. Sometimes I've been questioned about this. It seems odd to provide a positive send-off for someone who's resigning, but I actually see it differently. If we send the message that we appreciate your many years of service with us and we wish you well in your next job and there are no hard feelings, then everyone realizes we're a great place to work because we have such a positive outlook.

It actually creates a better reputation for the company. Often at The Sharper Image someone leaves and then later wants to come back and work for us again. I encourage us to take him or her back in. That's different from other companies, I realize, but again I think it makes our company look better. What could be better for the people who work at The Sharper Image than to know that Joe in accounting decided to leave us, and after working else-where for a year or two, wanted to come back? That's great! That's a wonderful endorsement of our company. We must be a good place to work because Joe checked out other companies and decided to come back to us a year later. That's a great result.

"Any publicity is good publicity, as long as they spell your name right."

P.T. Barnum said that. He was a famous promoter. Is it true? Probably, with some boundaries, it is true. It's great to be noticed and commented upon. That's certainly true in the world of entertainment and music. So many performers and stars have seen their careers take off after some outrageous piece of publicity. That happened in February 2004 at the Super Bowl with Janet Jackson and Justin Timberlake. I should point out that really negative publicity, especially when connected to some sort of criminal behavior, is not the sort of publicity one wants. That's not really anyone's wish.

In general, getting publicity for your business is a good thing. At The Sharper Image we've done a lot to cooperate with news television, entertainment television and others that want to come into our stores to film or tape, especially around the holiday season. Movie coverage is great if you can get it. The Sharper Image got one of its first meaningful exposures in the James Bond movie *A View to a Kill*, and later we got great exposure in a Billy Crystal movie called *When Harry Met Sally*. They shot a wonderful scene with Meg Ryan in a Sharper Image store in New York. This type of coverage is what you dream about in any business. We've also been mentioned many times on late-night talk shows such as Jay Leno or David Letterman, used in syndicated comic strips, or included in sitcoms on television like "Friends" or "Will & Grace."

How do you get coverage for your business? Consider doing something particularly charitable with a local organization. Perhaps you could host an event. You might do something wacky or off the wall, or maybe promote an unusual contest or a giveaway that's newsworthy. Make sure the local media is aware of it, of course.

Did you ever hear of a gas station selling gasoline at 1950s prices for 50 minutes at 11:50 p.m. on the last day of the year of the last century in 1999? I didn't either, but I suspect there would have been long lines to buy gas for 50 cents a gallon. That's probably worth a news story.

Certainly we all heard about Madonna kissing Britney Spears during the 2003 Music Video Awards in New York City. That was a kiss heard round the world. Think about what you can do. Be creative. Appearing in the local or national press is great for your business. See what you can do to get there.

A Visual History

FINALLY, A CHRONOGRAPH THAT KEEPS UP WITH AMAZING WALT STACK.

Walt Stack is an incredible man. He began running when he was 58. He is now 70 and has run 76 marathons, 9 fifty mile runs, and 1 one-hundred mile run. Each morning he bicycles 10 miles, runs 17 miles across the Golden Gate Bridge to Sausalito and back, jumps in the 50° salt water of the Bay for a half hour swim, then takes a half hour sauna at 200°. During all this morning activity he never takes off his Realtime Chronograph.

The Realtime Quartz Chronograph dramatically outdistances all watches in style, dependability and price. It was designed for active, athletic people like Walt, and now is available by mail from The Sharper Image for only $69 with ALL the following features.

MINIATURE TIME COMPUTER

In watch mode, it continually displays the hours, minutes, and seconds in large, easy to read liquid crystal numbers—without pressing buttons—even in direct sun.

The month, date and day of the week are immediately displayed with a touch of the side button. A night light is built in. The computer chip automatically adjusts for month end.

The Realtime weighs only 2.9 oz. with its stainless steel band or 1.5 oz. with a nylon band (not included). It has all the features you'll ever need in a watch or stopwatch, and is well protected by a slim stainless steel case.

TIME YOURSELF AND OTHERS

Record cumulative lap times. Splits. Switch to time of day and back. Take time out. And time beyond 60 minutes with automatic startover.

The stopwatch doesn't interfere with watch operation. Its quartz crystal vibrations split every second into 32,768 parts, making the Real-time more accurate than the finest mechanical chronograph ever made. You can time any event with precision to 1/100 of a second.

The Amazing Walt Stack

ACCURATE AND DURABLE

Unlike cheaper chronographs for the mass market, the Realtime Chronograph was built for rugged use. You can run and swim with it and not worry. If it can take the salt water of Walt's swimming, your perspiration won't harm it. It's water resistant down to 80 feet below the surface. The Realtime case and band are 100% stainless steel, not base metal or plastic. The face crystal is hard, scratch resistant rock glass, not plastic.

Accuracy is within 65 seconds a year. Its Union Carbide batteries last a year or more (unlike LED'S) and can easily be changed by your jeweler. Separate battery for night light gives you extra dependability and longer life.

MAINTENANCE FREE

Your Realtime has no moving parts and will probably never need service even after years of hard use. It carries a one year factory warranty on parts and labor. In the unlikely event it needs repair, prompt service by mail facilities are right here in the U.S.

ORDER WITHOUT OBLIGATION

We want you to be satisfied with your Realtime Chronograph. After you receive it, wear it. Compare it with any other chronograph. If for any reason it's not what you expected, return it within two weeks. You're guaranteed a full and courteous refund, with no questions asked.

PHONE NOW TOLL-FREE

Credit card holders will get fastest delivery by calling the toll-free number below. Or send check for $69 plus $1.50 delivery (add $4.14 sales tax in CA). But order now as supply is limited.

ORDER TOLL FREE

Ask for Operator 25R

(800) 824-5136

In California (800) 852-7631

THE SHARPER IMAGE

260 California Street
San Francisco, California 94111

An arresting headline and clear, interesting copy helped make this magazine ad our first one to really take off. It helped launch The Sharper Image in 1977.

The Sharper Image 1979 Catalog

This is the front cover of The Sharper Image 1979 Catalog, our first. It's hard to believe the graphics were so simple and clean.

HOW
TO BUILD A
GREAT
FORTUNE
IN
MAIL ORDER

A Complete Course
Covering All Phases
of the
Mail-Order
Business

v Gerardo Joffe

ume VII

An early publicity shot with the newest cordless phone and someone else's self-help book!

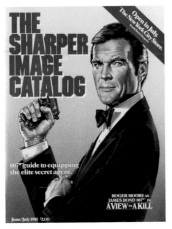

1985

1989

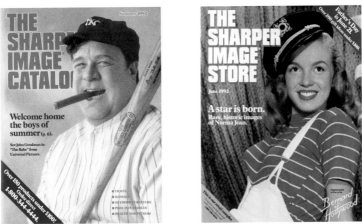

1992

1992

Celebrity covers have always been an important part of our culture and brand image.

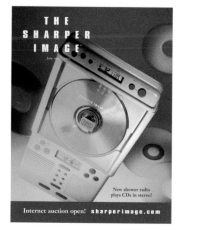

1999　　　　　　　　　**2001**

Catalog covers often feature new items "Invented Here" by Sharper Image Design, the company's own development group. In 1999, we introduced the first shower radio that plays CDs!

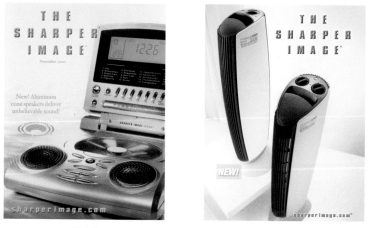

2002　　　　　　　　　**2004**

In 2004, we launched the new Professional Series™ Ionic Breeze®, an upgrade of the first air purifier that could circulate air without making any noise at all.

This was taken in 2001 at the grand opening of Sharper Image's 100th store, which happened to be in my hometown of Little Rock, Arkansas.

For more than 15 years, about two-thirds of Sharper Image's sales have come from retail stores in all kinds of different locations. Here's how our stores look today.

Sharper Image merchandising is fun and entertaining. This early appearance on the Merv Griffin Show featured a young Jay Leno in the back seat of one of our more eccentric products!

Meg Ryan and Billy Crystal in 1989's When Harry Met Sally. *Their long and funny scene in one of our Manhattan stores helped us become better known and made that store a favorite.*

Appearing with David Letterman was a special treat. David had a lot of fun with our products!

Sharper Image Corporation became a public company in 1987, 10 years after our founding. One benefit is that our management team had the opportunity to open the NASDAQ trading day on April 12, 2002.

Growing up in Little Rock provided a hometown connection to another Arkansas native, Bill Clinton, our 42nd president.

Here I am explaining the mail order business to His Royal Highness, the Prince of Wales.

Chapter 3

How to Work with People

What's the right starting salary when you're doing the hiring?

This is an interesting subject and there are a number of ways to approach it. Of course for entry-level positions it's determined fairly easily by checking around; no mystery there. For mid-level and higher it gets trickier. There aren't any hard and fast rules. It depends on so many variables. But let's talk first about hiring someone from the outside for a mid-level position.

If they've been working before they probably have a salary history, and assuming that their past salary history is in line with your expectations, my favorite approach is to ask this question, which might come up towards the end of the first or second job interview. "So, Doug, what do you think would be a fair starting salary for you in this position, with the understanding it will be reviewed again in 12 months? I mean, not the highest salary you'd like to get in your fantasy, but a realistic one that you think is fair in today's job market and with your skills, and also a reasonable number that makes sense for our company as well?"

I'm attempting to put Doug a little bit on the spot here. If he seriously gives me a number that is ridiculously high it makes him look bad, and he probably won't give me a number that's too low. Typically Doug would say he'd like to make, oh, let's just make something up, say $60,000. If that's acceptable to me, I'm always happy to be able to meet someone's expectations. If someone gets what they've asked for, they start off with a really positive attitude. You don't want them to come to work with a chip on their shoulder the first day.

If for some reason Doug gives me a number that's a bit too high, and I really don't want to offer that much, or if I want to test the waters, a polite approach might be: "Doug, that's in the ballpark, especially with your skills, and I'd really like to see you join us; however, I want to be honest and tell you there are some other candidates with similar or stronger experience, and they have a slightly lower salary request. Is it possible you would consider starting now at $50,000? That way you could get started with us today. With your skills and drive I expect you will do well and eventually you will get where you want to be."

This gives me a chance to see where he's at, and if he declines to come aboard for less I can always say, "Well, okay, let me mull it over. It is true you're asking for a bit more than we budgeted for this position, but we really think highly of you. Is there any other compromise between us that would work for you?" And if he still says no, I still have the option to say, "Well, fine, let me think it over. I really appreciate you and would like you to work with us. I'll call you tomorrow."

There's nothing wrong with letting it sit overnight, and then when you call the next day you can ask Doug if he still feels the same way, or if he's considered a compromise. If not, you can tell him, "You know, that's fine. I'm pleased to meet your number, Doug, because I want you to feel really positive about joining us, and I look forward to you starting soon."

The net result is you're going to find out Doug's bottom position, you're not going to lose face or embarrass yourself by checking to see where the bottom is, and at the same time you've left your options open to meet his number if you want. I think it's a very sound approach, and it'll work for you.

"Assume" makes an "ass" out of "u" and "me."

Think about it, the word "assume," A-S-S-U-M-E: "assume" makes an "ass" out of "u" and "me." What a silly saying! But hold on, this is a true saying! I'll bet that most of us have had the experience of assuming something was done, usually by somebody else, and then later finding out it hadn't been done, or it never happened. Most of the time, someone hasn't followed through.

If there's one simple rule to follow to ensure your success in business it is this one: **NEVER ASSUME.**

Follow up on everything that's really important to you. Most of the time we assign a task or we leave a message or send a request and assume it gets taken care of properly, but in real life it doesn't work that way. A substantial number of things just don't get done. At least they don't get done right away. Your follow-up will make a big difference in the speed and accuracy of the proper fulfillment of your requests.

Experienced managers know that to make sure something gets done, you must follow up. This isn't the same as doing it yourself. We all need to learn to delegate, but we multiply our effectiveness many times over by checking to see what was actually done and if it was completed. And don't get discouraged when you find out many times it's not done as you thought. This is human nature. We are not perfect, but we can follow up by making a phone call or sending an e-mail and asking someone if that particular project was done, or that call was returned.

So many times in my business or personal life I make one or two or three phone calls or e-mails before the other party responds. Maybe they're busy; maybe they have other clients or other deals. It isn't necessarily that they don't think I'm important enough. Maybe they know I'm a nice guy and that I'll wait and let them take care of something else first, or maybe they just don't know how to prioritize their work.

Humans are not robots; they don't always do things in the ideal order or on the priority schedule that suits you the best. So many times at work at The Sharper Image I ask somebody if they've reached Mr. Vendor to pursue a product that I asked them to look at. Sometimes what they say to me is, "I called, I left a message, they haven't called me back, we're still trading phone calls." And it's amazing how right then we'll pick up the phone, call them, and oddly enough they'll answer and we'll get the information we need. That happens about 75% or 85% of the time, even 90% of the time. Or Mr. Vendor says, "Gosh, that's funny. I've been calling you and waiting to get a call back."

That's the problem and the answer is so easy. Just follow up. It works. I'll venture most success in business is not because of being brilliant, but simply following up.

No one is irreplaceable, not even your computer programmer!

This is obviously one of the most challenging opportunities in business today. There are so many ways computers and software programs can help us, and at the same time so many ways they cause us grief and expense. I'll never forget years ago one of our most brilliant programmers, I'll call him Tony, had all the keys to our software in his head and he wasn't about to let any of us forget it!

He was a difficult person to work with. Of course he was totally smart and he knew it. He was also a bit conceited, sort of arrogant, sort of selfish, and unfortunately the only one that really knew what was going on with our software systems. It took about two years, but we finally decided we had had enough of his brilliance and his tantrums and we devised a strategy to build up enough bench strength around Tony that we were finally able to transition him out of the company. It was an arduous, time-consuming job, but finally Tony was gone. Man, were we happy.

From that point on I vowed that no one, regardless of how brilliant he was, would be the dominant person in our information technology area and we followed that.

Along the way we built lots of exclusive software and bought lots of expensive software. Software can be a money sink, and it will challenge you to decide where to put your resources. My approach may surprise you. In general I like to spend as little as possible, as slowly as possible. I'm not the type of manager who wants to jump in with both feet and purchase the latest program with all the bells and whistles at the highest price. My experience has shown me over time it really doesn't pay to be the first one to purchase the latest thing. It's just too fraught with expense and bugs.

During 1983 we put in a new order-processing system. We worked on it all summer. It was supposed to be ready in August, then it was going to be ready in September. In October it still wasn't working and we were almost into the Christmas selling season. The new software wasn't working, the old software wasn't going to be capable of handling the crush of orders, so we were about to have a disaster. There was no way we were going to be able to handle all those Christmas orders with the new system and we couldn't rely on the old system, so we were stuck in this gap between the old and the new. It was really going to be a problem.

Somehow at the last moment Leo, a wonderful computer consultant that I was working with, helped get it all working and it worked brilliantly. One might ask how did I (or more realistically, how did he), let it get so far behind schedule in the first place? Truthfully, that's the way it often is with new software projects. We were so fortunate that at the last minute it did work out. We got it working, we got through Christmas and we had a great year, but only by a narrow margin and only at the last minute. That's another experience that taught me never to put critical software in place without months and months of time to work out the bugs.

People like to know how they fit into the overall business picture.

You've noticed in your own job how you enjoy so much more being asked to do something if it's accompanied by a magic word. "Jim, would you please take this down to the first floor? I'd really appreciate it." You might call it good manners, but it goes a long way. People really don't like to be treated as cogs in a business machine. They want to be respected and treated as individuals. Whether it's a fancy top floor office or a warehouse packing floor, you see the same problem every day. The boss sometimes forgets that a lower ranking person has feelings too.

You should personally treat everyone with a lot of human respect and courtesy and professionalism, and encourage those you work with to do the same thing. Of course this is also true when dealing with others you encounter in the course of your business day. Whether it's on the phone or in person, calling someone "sir" or saying "yes, ma'am" gets you a lot further toward your goal.

One step beyond showing respect and courtesy to your associates is to explain why you're asking them to do a particular task. "Jerry, could you please pack this mail order first? If we can get it on the UPS trailer within the hour it may help prevent a customer service call later, because the customer will receive it one day sooner."

In other words, it's great to get your associates to do what you want, but it's even better to be educating them at the same time as to the reason behind your request. You'll be combining training and accomplishing a task at the same time. And of course you'll notice who's getting it, who's picking up on the training and the logic behind the requests. It's an easy way for you to achieve better relations with everyone, accomplish more projects, and at the same time identify and train your future supervisors.

There is so much for people to learn about doing their job better, and about how their job relates to other departments in the company. Each time you give someone direction you can share your knowledge of how it all fits together. In my interactions with people at work there are so many opportunities to share information about our business; why some ideas are good, and others perhaps are not. It's a fruitful combination of a working relationship and a teaching relationship.

Understanding the big picture and the small details.

You often work with a manager or a supervisor who reports to you and supervises others. Sometimes the supervisor doesn't know or understand the details involved in the work being performed by those he or she supervises. This situation is a real red flag. I expect the manager, or the supervisor, not only to have a big-picture grasp of his or her job, but also to know quite a bit about all the details involved. You shouldn't let them repeatedly tell you, as people have told me over the years, "Oh, I don't know that detail, but I can find out and get back to you." If you hear that line too many times you should wake up and take action.

Clearly every manager doesn't know everything that everybody is doing. On the other hand, if you repeatedly ask them for details about projects they're supervising and they consistently don't know them, my belief is he or she is not adequately detail-oriented. I've seen it happen too many times. I'll bet you 10 dollars it's the same in your business, too. People either know the big picture as well as the small picture, or they don't know enough to manage effectively.

I'll never forget one executive that worked for me in the early years. Dave was a competent manager in many respects, but he didn't spend a lot of time worrying about the details of the department he was supervising. We used to go back and forth about this. I'd keep reminding him he could really help me by taking care of, or at least having detailed knowledge of, everything going on in his department.

I'll never forget his reply. He told me I worried too much about the details, and he really should be focusing on the big picture. I listened and then I remember calmly telling him, "No, actually, Dave, you should be focusing on the details, and if you would, then I could focus on the big picture and I'd be able to quit worrying so much about the details."

Needless to say, Dave and I didn't last too much longer. I think he went on to a successful career with another company where he could focus on the big picture and leave the details to others.

The best team has complementary players.

It's interesting that sometimes the best working company has most diverse work force. At The Sharper Image we are a widely disparate group. Our ethnicity, backgrounds, geographical origin, almost everything widely varies across our ranks, and this has made for a great mix of people. We started with the principle that we tolerate absolutely no sexism, racism, discrimination or any other "isms" for any reason, and that's a great foundation.

It's become apparent that along the way we developed a culture that prizes and values respect for others, courtesy, evenhanded approaches to promotions and raises, and a general camaraderie that's contagious. We make an effort to have regular gatherings to communicate what's going on in the company, as well as social events to give everyone a chance to meet and talk with people from other departments at all levels. Needless to say, elitism of any sort isn't our style.

It turns out that mixing a wide range of people with complementary skills has been a sound approach to hiring and staffing. It really works for us. And one more observation: The people we hire tend to have lives outside of work. Many are parents, some have hobbies or exercise regularly, but all tend to have lives outside of work. That's probably one of the reasons they bring fresh energy and experience to their jobs. What's the moral? Embrace different types of people, mix personalities, find complementary types of people, and make sure they all get to know each other and respect each other. Never tolerate backbiting or office politics. You'll be very pleased with the results.

Praise in public and criticize in private.

Have you heard this before? It's just about the briefest and best management advice ever written. Following this advice will give you better odds of being successful and well-liked as a manager. When you criticize in private it is important to avoid emotion. After all, the objective of criticizing in private is to get a beneficial result from the conversation. The point is not to hurt someone's feelings or their ego. If you make the conversation unpleasant, nasty, or personal, they'll be thinking about the hurt instead of thinking about how they can learn from the situation.

Your mission is to keep the conversation polite, calm and objective. Talk about what you need to get accomplished and how they can help you accomplish it. Talk about specifics such as work performance, job objectives and techniques, alternative methods to achieve optimal work performance. Let's not insult the person's abilities. That won't help. You want to get them on your side, to get them moving in the direction you want. If the relationship ultimately is not going to work out, then a verbal warning may be the first step. This may lead to future verbal and eventually written warnings.

However, there's no reason the conversation shouldn't be matter of fact, even-tempered and calm, even when delivering a warning. Some very successful executives are known for their volatile tempers, their yelling and screaming; however, I don't see how that could ever be helpful. You want a reputation for being even-tempered and positive. People love to be praised, and you should be free with your compliments. Praising in public goes a long way.

Moving someone out of a job can be a positive step for both of you.

I don't find many people that are good at delivering negative news to someone they're supervising. Whether it's a job termination, rejecting a vendor's product idea or giving a verbal warning, it's so important to leave the person feeling as positive as possible. It makes you feel better for one thing, it definitely makes them feel better, and hopefully it gets them going in the right direction with an uplifted spirit. They'll like you better for it, and who knows, they may be back someday with a great idea or in a different capacity. Besides, it's good karma to spread positive energy.

Consider this cold example. "Mike, I'm sorry, your work has not measured up. You've received three verbal warnings and three written notices. You just haven't cut it. I have no choice but to fire you. Good-bye, Mike."

Now let's try a much more positive and constructive approach: "Mike, I know you've tried your best. It's unfortunately still not meeting the minimum requirements for this position; however, you really are an interesting and talented person. This probably is not the right position for you. You need to find something you enjoy doing in order for you to succeed. That's why I'm removing you from this position. But let's look on the bright side. You're heading up from here, seriously, because tomorrow we're both going to wake up feeling better and you'll think, 'Hey, I'm going to find a job I really enjoy and it will be great.' Meanwhile, the company will find someone better suited for the job. Everyone has a talent or an area they excel in. Just because this wasn't it doesn't mean you're not really going to succeed. It just means you need to find a position where you're going to be successful. You'll see. Thanks, Mike."

Of course you have to use your own language, but in this kind of interview it's very important to show respect and concern. Seriousness is appropriate. Anyone losing his or her job is naturally worried. However, you demonstrated your sincere belief that Mike is a good human being, a capable individual, and when he finds the right job he will excel. You can convey that with sincerity.

It's a great help to move someone in a positive direction. If they're working at something they're not good at or not interested in, they aren't fulfilling themselves and they won't prosper, so you really are helping them move toward success. Feel totally good about yourself in that role. Be positive with them and send them off in the right direction.

What are people really working for?

People work for a lot of reasons. Obviously they work for money, that's a big reason; but let's not overlook other reasons as well. Many people work because they love what they do; they work because they get recognition and it satisfies their ego to be recognized. There's nothing wrong with that at all, as long as you as a manager realize it's not always about the money.

Sometimes there are fringe benefits that make a job appealing. Certainly a title or a nice office with a window goes a long way toward satisfying people. For others the opportunity to work from home one day a week is a terrific benefit. It's interesting in today's work environment, with Internet access, e-mail, cell phones and voice mail, it often doesn't matter where you work. For those with long commutes to the office, you may find they would rather stay at home on

Friday, avoid the long commute and use e-mail and phone instead. Quite frankly you may find they get more done if they're not spending an hour a day sitting in their car. This doesn't work for everybody, but for some this is a huge benefit.

There are other intangibles that are also motivating and lead to something tangible. Stock shares or stock options in the company are a great incentive. Many employees are motivated by getting a piece of the action and enjoy the pride of ownership that comes with being a part owner, even if it's only a small part. Many people enjoy working for a company like ours that encourages a healthy family life with time for exercise and outside activities. There are so many intangibles that go into making one's work life a satisfying one. Your job is to discover the various benefits that make working more enjoyable and meaningful and provide these benefits as much as possible to your associates. If there's one thought above all others that has guided me and can help you, it's to encourage you to remember to speak and think of others working "with you," not "for you." This makes a big difference in attitude and respect. It makes a healthy relationship even better. People may spend more time at work than they spend with their family. You want to make their time at work as pleasant as possible. Everyone will do a better job and accomplish more.

Treat people with respect.

You've got to forgive me for repeating this since we've touched on it so many places, but it's so important it's worth repeating. It's important to treat everyone with respect. It doesn't matter who it is. It can be the receptionist on the phone at your lawyer's office, it can be the receptionist on the phone at the pool maintenance company, it can be the counter help at the local burrito takeout place, or the ticket seller at your neighborhood movie theater.

No matter who it is, the constant effort to charm them will not only make you incredibly popular, you'll get a lot of practice displaying great manners and a wonderful personality, and because you'll practice so much, you're going to get really good at being charming. The more you practice the better you'll get.

Soon you'll charm anyone, anytime, and how great is that? Now when you want to get that entrée into an office, or need a favor from someone, you'll turn on the charm effortlessly. What a great asset this is for you to have. All it takes is consistency with everyone you meet or talk to. It helps to like people, and it will make you happy to see how happy you can make others. It really is a great way to go through the day.

Try it tomorrow. Spend your entire day being charming to a phone operator, a clerk in a store, a waiter, a parking lot attendant. It's sometimes challenging to get a smile out of others, but try it. You'll probably have a lot of fun, and even when you're being critical, it's more fun and more productive to do it with respect.

I had an interesting experience in someone else's store the other day. I asked the store manager to make an exception on a product exchange, which she didn't want to do. I said, "You know, I completely understand. You're doing your job and you're doing it well. You're following company policy and I completely understand that. Who can I contact that's higher up and has the authority to make this exception? Would you give me their name and phone number?"

Well, that did it. The combination of being polite and respectful, coupled with the message that I would need to speak to someone in authority did the trick. I don't know if it was her pride that made her want to prove she had the authority, or if she didn't want her boss to get a complaint about her store. Regardless, she suddenly decided to do what I was requesting. I thanked her profusely and I told her I was going to write to the head of the company and say what a terrific manager she was. We definitely catch more flies with honey than vinegar!

Why, and how, businesses change.

Just like people, businesses change over time. The small business that I started originally had just me and one other. A year or two later there was me and three other employees. A year or so later there were 10 of us. A few years went by and there were 25 people. Today The Sharper Image has almost 4,000 associates.

It changed along the way in many different respects. The point is that things do change and so do the required resources. Many of the skills that were required when we started were not the same skills required when we passed $100 million in sales and they're not the same skills required when we passed $500 million in sales.

So what exactly are we talking about? This is pretty simple in theory, but hard to implement in practice. The theory goes like this. When you start, you need people around you who get things done. These are the fast, get it done, "doer" types. They're the take-charge, type-A people. Surprisingly though, about 10 years later the people that were so good at getting things done were now sometimes getting in the way. Maybe they didn't like working as a team, maybe they had problems delegating, maybe they were incapable of learning to supervise others, or, to make it worse, they didn't want to be supervised themselves.

So keep your eyes open and manage the transition. You'll need to be prepared that as the business grows, the needs of the business and the resources required also change. Getting it done is still important, only now it's an entire team that has to work together. Having one star player on a team is not the best way. You probably know that from watching sports, especially basketball. It's better to have a team that works well together, likes each other, shares the glory of success and avoids backbiting and office politics.

There's a temptation to treat our business like our favorite pair of comfortable shoes. We'd like to wear them forever, but times change. Don't be surprised when you eventually need to get a new pair. The life of every business is filled with transition periods, sometimes painful transitions, but that's the way it's going to be. There will always be moments when things go smoothly and times when the waters seem way too choppy. That's just the nature of life and business.

Everyone has heard that change is inevitable and nothing stays the same. That's the way it's always been. The earth does not stop changing; we have not stopped changing. Some people have difficulty coping with change and some people more easily cope with it. Most entrepreneurs are comfortable with a changing situation and are ready to adapt to it.

67

You'll do even better with a great "right-hand" person.

My business has had years that were easier than others and years that were difficult, but when I had a really great right-hand person helping me, the business was so much easier to grow. Most of us have either a creative side or an administrative side.

I like to think I can do both well, but in reality it's more productive to focus on one or the other. However, once you decide to focus on the creative side, you're going to need someone to administer the everyday details. And if you decide to be the operations-oriented person, you're going to need someone to focus on creativity, marketing and sales campaigns.

By the way, a mismatched right-hand person can be a real drag. You'll argue and struggle over who's doing what, who gets to make the decisions, and a lot of negative energy is created. I remember some years like that at The Sharper Image. I spent a lot of time on assorted issues that were not really productive.

During last few years our president and chief operating officer, Tracy Wan, has made an incredible contribution to our company. She has made the business so much better and stronger and we have grown faster than ever in our history. Do your best to find that type of person to help you; you'll be so glad you did.

The challenge is to find the type of person that helps you, supports you and complements your skills so you can focus on what you want and they'll take care of the rest. That's the ideal match. Of course, they can't aspire to take over your functions; that would be nonproductive. This is a common conflict in smaller businesses, but you'll figure it out over time. Look for that complementary person and you'll do so much better.

Who's really running your business?

This is an interesting problem that comes up regularly as a business grows. It occurs especially in smaller, growing businesses. If you started the business you assume you're the boss; that's natural. Eventually you hire someone as a right-hand person and it often works out great. Other times, before you know it, they'll begin acting like they're the boss and you're an extra appendage. This is not good.

Believe me, this almost always happens if you stay in business long enough. Sometimes as the company gets bigger it happens just within a department. After awhile the person the vice president of merchandising hired to be the second in command is attempting to take over the leadership of the department. Your vice president will be coming to you asking for support to rein in the new number two who's aspiring to be the number one in that department.

Sometimes it's healthy to let the friction evolve for a week or two. Perhaps it shakes up a stagnant group that needs some new ideas, but eventually you're going to have to make a tough decision to control the newly aggressive number two, or risk losing number one, or watch the department become chaotic or paralyzed.

This situation can sometimes be used to help push out a stagnant number one in a department that needs shaking up. It's a weak way to address it, but people do it. A better approach is to figure out a way that the newly aggressive number two can have a completely separate area of responsibility.

Sometimes you just have to tell the newly aggressive number two that it's not going to work out the way it's going and they have a choice. They can either play with the team, support the coach or leave. They simply cannot continue to create subversion and chaos. Usually if this message is delivered fairly and honestly it will be well received. Let them know that if they can demonstrate a consistent performance they will eventually get their fair share and move up the ladder.

A version of this problem occurs when you have someone in place as head of a department and the business has grown. Now you want to bring in a more expensive hire with more substantial experience. The former number one will now report to the new number one, hired from outside the company. This is a tough situation and often doesn't work out. The best way to deal with it is to sit down with the former department head, explain that the business has grown and it's time to bring in more talent. Tell them you hope they'll stay and work for the new person.

It helps to view this situation as a reorganization of the department with new titles for both the old number one and the new number one. If the old number one gets a salary increase at the same time the promotion is being announced, the waters will remain a lot calmer. That turns what was perceived as an ego blow into a transitional ego boost. That's a better result for everyone.

People obviously have a lot of pride in what they do, and you don't want to create the impression that the old number one couldn't make it. Instead, announce that the company has grown, the department is being enlarged and reorganized and then introduce the redesigned structure.

Managing people's expectations and keeping them on a career track that works for your business.

This has to be the best topic ever. Anyone who runs a small or medium-sized business knows this is one of the important keys to building a company. Let's start with the obvious fact. People want to be respected, liked and listened to. Regular communication goes a long way, even those one-minute, one-on-one chats that give you a chance to ask about someone's family, how their daughter is doing at a school or how they enjoyed their recent vacation.

Short, personal (but not too personal) conversations keep you in touch with the human side of the people you work with. Every month or so you want to check in with them. Perhaps invite them to your office or drop into their office and let them know how things are going from your point of view. Ask for their thoughts. What I like to do is ask, "Hey, Mark, what do you like best about your job? What do you like least about your job? I'd like to hear because I want to know how you're doing and how we can make it better for you."

You might say, "Are you enjoying what you're doing? If you could delegate something, some sort of drudgework, what part would that be?" I always mention I'd like to make their job as enjoyable as possible.

Of course we all have some drudgework; I certainly do. My whole life has been filled with drudgework, but only if Mark tells me what part of his job he doesn't like can I begin to think about how to change it. It's really important to me to know if Mark is enjoying doing the parts of his job that need to be done. If he isn't, then I have to think about this.

What if Mark is telling me that the part of his job he doesn't like is the one aspect that's most important to me? Then I have to think about either moving Mark into a job he'd like better, or I have to think about replacing him with somebody who really likes doing that job.

It's also valuable to ask directly, "By the way, where do you imagine yourself being in a year from now or two years from now? Where do you want to be?" This gives you an accurate and more reliable picture about what they're really thinking. If you think the person's moving in a direction that works for your company, that's great; you'll be glad to have the information to help move them along.

If you don't see them moving in a positive direction, then you'll realize there's a real disconnect. They want to move in one direction; you want them to stay where they are or do something else. You'll have to begin planning for a later replacement down the road or formulate a plan to remedy the situation. All in all, having this information helps you plan your business. You'll be able to decide who's going to be doing this job in a year and who's going to be helping you. It's invaluable information.

Chapter 4

How to Negotiate a Better Deal

How to negotiate positively and still find the bottom.

There are many advice books on this subject, so I won't pretend to be an expert. On the other hand, there is a simple, understandable technique that's worked for me, and it's easy for you to use it, too. It starts with the premise that you always want to compliment the other side, even when you're about to ask for a significant concession, or a better price, or for them to give something up.

If you insult them, or tear down their reputation, or cause them to lose face — especially if it's done in front of other people — you make it difficult for the other side to give in. Either they're too preoccupied with their own hurt feelings to pay attention to you, or they lose face in front of their colleagues and are now not in the mood to hand you what you want. So keep it as positive as you can as you lead up to your request. Tell them how much you appreciate the product they supply, or the great business relationship the two of you have had in the past and can have in the future.

Having laid a positive foundation for good spirits and mutual ego building, go to step two. Explain that regardless of how good the product is, or that you know "it's an expensive process that produces a quality product," the simple fact is "we will do a lot more business together, and our relationship will continue to be successful only if we can get to the pricing point that lets it work for both of us."

How do we do that? Again, emphasize the issue is not that their product isn't worth what they want to charge for it. That isn't the point. The point is that you want to make it work and it isn't going to work as well at that price, you're not going to be able to sell as many, etc.

Now we've accomplished two things. We've started the conversation on a positive note by building them up, not tearing them down. And two, we've explained it's necessary to get a better price or term concession. Not because they're wrong in any way, but because you want to maximize overall sales and unit volume for both of you, and that change is necessary to get there.

Last but not least, there's an effective way to close this negotiation. You want to find out where the bottom is in your request without causing them to lose face or closing off the possibility for future requests. It might sound like this: "Mr. Vendor, thanks for offering to lower the price 5% and waive the shipping costs. That's a great concession. It means a lot to me. It shows what an effort you're making. However, I should ask if there are other areas of flexibility on your part. Not that you haven't already offered a lot, but because I really want us to be successful together on this, and the sweeter the deal, the more we can promote the product. It's that simple. Is that it, or can you go a bit further to make this work?"

If they say no, you can still respectfully and politely approach this from another direction with the same objective. You might say, "Okay, I get the point. There's not a single penny more to be reduced in price, I got that, but are there some other areas that will add to the overall attractiveness of the contract that we might work on? For example, what about display units? Can you provide us with some display units at no cost? Or what about returns? We've been paying all the cost of returns. Can you pick that cost up? That would help sweeten the deal."

Is it beginning to sound like I'm nagging the vendor? That's not my objective; I don't want to nag. It has to be done in a polite way, not with constant wheedling or whining, but the deal should be approached in several ways from several different directions. You want to find out how much more can be added. In other words, where is the bottom? Last but not least, I actually don't like to squeeze that last drop out of the negotiation. Instead, I want to leave a little bit on the table.

Negotiations should be a win-win for both of you.

I really believe the best negotiation is one in which you get the best deal possible for you, but you don't want the worst deal possible for the other party either. That's not a good result. Let me clarify this. First, this entire discussion only applies when you're dealing with suppliers and vendors that are smaller than you, or are your equal. If you're dealing with a bank or a large vendor like IBM, take whatever you can get. These businesses don't need any help from you!

However, when dealing with smaller vendors, distributors, manufacturers or service providers, they will often go overboard, even to the point of under-pricing their goods. This is not necessarily a good thing for you. The fact that they're not making the profit margin they need will eventually be reflected in the end result. They'll make up the shortfall by putting your order last, or by cutting quality control, or substituting slightly inferior goods or services. That's just the way it is.

There really isn't any way for them to cut their pricing to you below their minimum without something having to give, or some corner being cut. There's an important psychological component to the relationship as well. Like any human relationship, both parties need to respect each other and do a good job. It's hard for them to deliver the extra quality and effort for you when you squeeze them too hard — and they know it.

Think about how it can beneficially change their attitude if, after you've pushed them to get the very best price, you voluntarily lighten up and give them back a little in the deal. What do they think of you? They think you're generous, fair, reasonable and the type of partner they want to do business with. That's great! Now they're really going to work for you, give you their full attention and perform their best.

When we introduced our new electric cruiser bike in the summer of 2003, our manufacturing vice president complained that the factory wasn't very responsive. They were slow; they couldn't commit to delivery dates. Eventually I learned the real issue. They were losing money on every unit. No wonder they didn't want to commit to future orders; no wonder they were dragging their feet. Ultimately, we agreed to pay them about 10% more and all of a sudden they were again responsive and eager to please us.

A lot of people think they must absolutely get the very best deal, but surprise, it's not really that way. You want to accomplish an overall result. Price is part of the overall picture, but there's also performance, quality, delivery and the quality of the relationship that are the most important parts of the equation. You want to make sure everybody wins.

The only time to negotiate is when you don't care if you get it.

This technique is for those times when you want to get best deal possible and that's all that matters. For instance when you buy a new car or house, a building, or a new computer. This is not a relationship-building exercise. This is simply a cold-blooded, best-deal negotiation, and nothing more!

The approach is very simple. Arrange the timing of the negotiation for when you're not feeling pressured to close the deal. A typical example would be leasing an office space at a time when you really don't need it, or applying for a loan you don't really need, or making an offer on a car when you really don't want to buy it. In other words, you feel no pressure whatsoever to make any particular deal. This is the key part of the approach.

Basically, you're going to respond to every offer with this response: "That sounds pretty good; I think we're making progress. Is there further room for improvement? I'd like to sleep on it overnight and get back to you." Later in the conversation you're going to wrap it up this way: "I appreciate how far you've come; that's a terrific deal. You know, it's still a bit higher than what I had in mind. Let me see if I can put this together in my mind and I'll get back to you. Thanks so much for your time." Then leave the negotiating table or leave the office and just walk out.

One of two things will happen at this point. The other side will stop you from leaving and offer you a sweeter deal; or two, you'll leave and perhaps call them back in an hour or a day to let them know you've thought it over and decided to accept their offer.

The worst thing that can happen in this situation is that you will not get the deal you want, but the premise of this negotiation is that you don't care whether you get it or not anyway. You either get the best possible deal or you don't make a deal at all. If you've fallen in love with the deal at this point and allowed your emotions to get involved, that's a different situation. It happens all the time, usually when you're house shopping or car shopping! Try to remember not to get emotionally committed to an outcome when you go into the negotiation.

This is a technique that works because you don't care whether you get it or not. Keep telling yourself that! It makes the negotiation so much fun. The other side cares and you don't! Keep it that way throughout the negotiation and you'll get some terrific deals.

Negotiating ploys you shouldn't fall for.

You may have heard these before, but they come up so often it's worth mentioning the techniques that other people will try on you. You definitely don't want to get sucked in by them. They're negotiating techniques that are designed to do nothing but close the deal for the other side.

Here are the pitches, and the responses you should give. One you'll often hear is, "What price do you have in mind?" Don't get pushed into disclosing your price unless you lowball it by a very wide margin. You know there's a good chance that if you throw out a price that's acceptable to you, the other side may well grab your hand and congratulate you on closing the deal. But you're left wondering, how much did I leave on the table? Don't disclose your price; let them disclose theirs. If they ask, just tell them, "You know, I really don't know what it's worth to me today. I just need to reflect on it."

Here's another technique they'll try on you: "If I can meet that price can we close the deal today?" Again, don't answer yes unless you are positively sure you want the deal and are satisfied you've reached the rock bottom price. It's obvious you're put in the position of having accepted the deal or the other side would not have used the phrasing to close it that way. Tell them that even if both of you make a deal today, you still need to get approval from your boss or your bank or your partner. In other words, leave yourself some sort of "out." Blaming it on your husband or wife is a very good excuse. Tell the other party you really like the deal but you can't say yes until you get your partner's agreement.

A terrific line you should always use is this: "Mr. Vendor, this is a really terrific offer you've made. I appreciate it so much. However, I promised Mr. Vendor Number Two that I wouldn't make a final decision until I meet with them one more time. I promise I won't use your price against them, because I believe in keeping your bid in confidence, but I still owe it to myself and my company to hear their best price as well. Let me get back to you as soon as I've had a chance to talk with them." You may quickly get a better price from vendor number one in that situation.

When you've gotten final prices from your vendors and chosen the one you're ready to accept, try saying to them, "Mr. Vendor, your bid is great, I like it a lot and I know we're going to have a growing and productive business relationship in the future. This is just the beginning of what I hope will be a lot more business. Now, before I accept the price and let the other vendors know that they're about to lose out on this, let me ask one more time just to make sure. Is this really your best offer or is there a little bit more room to make it slightly sweeter?" Then stop talking, just be quiet, don't say a word, and wait for them to respond. If they say it's the absolute rock bottom price, then you politely reply, "I understand. Thanks for giving it one more look. Let's shake hands and make a deal." If they come back and say, "Well, we can knock another 2% off if you pay us in 30 days," then you can reply, "I understand. Thanks for giving it one more look. Let's shake hands and make a deal."

In summary, so much of negotiation is learning how to politely, and with respect, find out where the bottom of the negotiation is without insulting the other side, without hurting their feelings or sounding cheap. It's an art well worth learning.

Chapter 5

Advertising Effectively

The mystery of advertising.

Forgive me for badly paraphrasing an axiom about advertising: "We know half of our advertising is really working and half of it isn't. The only problem is we don't know which half is which." Sound familiar? Most advertising is "display" advertising, which simply means it displays the product or the service; there's no ordering mechanism attached to the ad. Ads for Gap khaki pants on television, most cosmetic ads, and most automobile ads are considered display advertising. They show the product and try to motivate you to buy the product or service.

What some companies use, and at The Shaper Image we use it exclusively, is "direct response" advertising. This means our ads have some sort of response mechanism built in, usually in the form of a call to action, encouraging the consumer to actually order the product. This can be a toll-free phone number, a Website address or a mail-in coupon. You've seen lots of these, so you know what I'm talking about. Direct response advertising gives the customer an opportunity to place an order.

The advantage of this type of advertising is huge. We attach a source code to each and every ad, usually with a unique order number or something similar, and this allows us to accurately track the actual performance of the ad. How does one magazine ad compare to another? How does one newspaper ad compare to another? Now you have hard evidence, which is worth your investment.

In an ideal world you'd like every dollar of advertising to pay back the cost of the ad and also make a profit for you. For example, if the ad costs a hundred dollars, you'd want to get back your hundred dollars plus something extra to cover your overhead: office rent; coworkers' salaries; etc. If you could do that every time, you'd literally be making money out of thin air.

Every time you place an ad you want to recover the money you paid for it; you want to get back enough money to cover the cost of the product, or the cost of the service you're giving away, plus expenses. Once you recover the cost of the ad, your expenses and some profit, you're ahead of the game. You haven't lost a penny. In fact, you've made money. And not only have you made money, you've advertised your business. You just got free advertising!

Simple enough? That's the formula we use. Over the years it's grown into a bigger advertising expense but we still use the same formula. Advertising expenses for us in 2004 will reach approximately $140 million, clearly a lot more than the initial $250 that my first ad cost back in 1977, but the principle is exactly the same. Managing the return on investment in advertising is what it's all about. This is the only way you can tell which half of the advertising is working.

The biggest businesses like IBM, Gap, Microsoft, General Motors or Nike are not worrying so much about every ad placement. They've already committed millions of dollars for advertising and they're perfectly content to spend the money on flashy display ads that promote their brand. That makes sense for them. They still don't necessarily know which half of their advertising is working, but they can do sophisticated follow-up consumer research to ask customers where they saw the ad, what they remember about it and so on.

We don't have that luxury. We need to watch our dollars more carefully, and if you're in a start-up mode you definitely want to get every benefit from every dollar you spend. Your goal now is to apply your creativity to direct response tracking techniques for your ads. It can be very simple. For example, "Bring in this ad for a free dessert with your meal," or "Show this ad and receive a free gift with your purchase," or "Mention this ad and you'll receive a 10% discount on your first order." All of these approaches work because the most important thing is to know which advertising placements are the most successful. Then you're really on the road to rapidly growing your business.

How much should you spend on advertising?

Here's another interesting mystery about advertising. Let me describe the scenario. You start a business and the first year you budget $2,000 a month for advertising. Maybe that buys you some newspaper ads, some direct mail circulars, a magazine ad or maybe a placement on a Web search engine. Sound okay? Now consider a similar idea but bigger. Let's say you could spend $20,000 a month instead of $2,000, and to make sure you sleep at night, pretend I'll throw in a guarantee that you won't lose any money doing it. You may not make much profit on the extra advertising, but let's make the decision easy by assuring you there will be no risk of financial loss.

But let's go one better. How about we spend $200,000 a month on advertising your business instead? That's right, it adds up to $2.4 million a year. Wow, that's a lot of advertising! You'd better stock up on whatever you're selling with that kind of advertising muscle! Oh yeah, let's not forget, we still want you to sleep at night, so to make sure you do, I'll repeat the earlier guarantee. You may not make any extra profit, but you'll get back everything you spent plus a little to cover all those incremental expenses.

Does this sound too good to be true? Perhaps. I'm a few years ahead of where you are right now, but that's the vision, the picture, the goal. You want to spend as much as possible on advertising your business, and why not? It will only bring you more name recognition, more sales, more customers, more market share and more new business. All you have to do is make sure you break even or make money doing it and that there's no substantial risk of losing money on your advertising. So how much should you spend on advertising? The answer should be to spend as much as you can; build it up over time and make sure you're getting back your investment. As long as you're confident that each ad placement is going to give you a payback, be as aggressive as you can. You'll build your business even faster!

What makes an advertisement work?

I suppose we should define "work." For me, advertising works when it stops you with the headline, makes you curious enough to read it, then motivates you to place an order or go to a Website. Stopping you is the first part, and it's the most fun and challenging. It's invariably a combination of a headline and a picture, at least in print ads, though sometimes no picture is required. Regardless, it must be a grabber. Often short headlines are good but there's no hard and fast rule. Photos work better when you're selling a benefit like a beautifying hair shampoo, but words work better when selling a new technical feature.

Regardless, the rule is simple: You must grab the reader or the viewer, capture their attention for a millisecond, and intrigue them enough to get them to read (or watch) the body of the ad.

And what's in the ad? In my view, simple paragraphs broken up with subheads and fairly simple sentences, even incomplete sentences or phrases. Like this one.

Every subhead should continue the story on its own. In other words, if the reader only reads the headline and all the subheads, that should be a compelling sales story in itself. The short paragraphs between the subheads are there to connect the story and fill it in, and it should be a fast and easy read.

One of my favorite lessons in life came to me from an accomplished trial lawyer. He told me, "It should be said with language that every single person on the jury can understand." In other words, language that's difficult for some to understand, or vocabulary choices that demonstrate your ability, are not what effective advertising is about.

It's easier to convey a point with long-winded, wordy presentations; it's much harder to say the same thing in fewer, simpler words that everyone understands. But that's your goal: as simple, as compelling, as spare as possible.

Don't waste a word, because they all cost you money in advertising. Every word saved is an opportunity to say more.

My favorite words in advertising.

My favorite word is any variation of the word "you," as in, "You are sure to be pleased with the new Ionic Breeze Silent Air Purifier." I'm also quite fond of the word "satisfied," as in, "Your satisfaction is guaranteed." When I was a child growing up in Little Rock, Arkansas, my family was in the department store business. Over every store exit was a big sign that read, "Every customer must be satisfied." That slogan made a lasting impression on me and I've tried to carry that with me every day.

Another word I like a lot, even though we see it so often, is "free." Everyone likes something for free, don't they? I probably have more favorite words, but these are the four magic words in much successful advertising:

You

Satisfied

Free

Now

For example, "Now you can get this free offer, and you're sure to be satisfied." Using those words in the ad somewhere will produce results. You may say, Gosh, they've been overused; they've been used in so many advertisements in so many ways.

Your challenge then is to make your advertisement interesting, creative, original, and still use some of those words. You'll be pleased that you did, and "I promise you'll be satisfied."

Words to avoid in advertising.

The words I avoid most are "I" or "we." That's because of my belief that anyone reading an ad wants to know what's "in it for them." So if I say to you, "I think this is one of our best offers," that will probably not motivate you as much as if I said, "You are getting the best offer." Or compare these two: "Our new catalog has lots of terrific gifts in it," with this alternative, "You're going to find lots of terrific gifts in this new catalog."

Are you beginning to see my point? It's also the same in business letters. Consider the starting paragraph of a typical business letter: "Dear Mr. Jones, I know you'll be impressed with the presentation I'll be showing you."

Now let's rewrite it using more of a "you" orientation: "Dear Mr. Jones, You're going to be impressed with the presentation you'll be seeing." Not only is the second version quicker; it immediately focuses on the benefit to the recipient. You can take this on faith. The reader usually doesn't care much what you think; rather, they want to know "what's the benefit for them."

The more you orient your thoughts in this direction, the sooner your message will be received and accepted. Of course this is also true in all types of verbal communication. Consider something as simple as a job interview. Would you rather interview someone who's talking about what they think and what they want, or would you rather interview someone who's interested in how your company can match up with their skills, how they can make a contribution to your company, and how you can benefit from hiring them?

The answer is pretty obvious. The orientation may seem like a bit of wordsmithing, but it's deeper than that. It's the very essence of good persuasion and good selling. Try it and you'll see the results right away!

Four ways to price your product or service.

There are only four ways that I know of to price a product or service. They all have different reasons for being and apply at different times, and each is perfectly understandable. The first is a market share approach. This has nothing to do with anything other than wanting to be priced low enough so that the consumer chooses to buy your product, and therefore you grab market share.

This is how Lexus automobile got started and carved out a substantial niche in the luxury car market. They deliberately priced their flagship Lexus, when it was introduced, at about $35,000, which was at that time about $10,000 less than comparable offerings from BMW or Mercedes. Their strategy was to entice a lot of people to buy their car because of the attractive price. They didn't worry about whether they made or lost money. They knew they had to get their cars out on the road, in people's garages and generate positive word of mouth. Then they could raise prices years later once they got established. Of course it helped that the cars were great quality. The strategy worked well for them. It's a classic market share approach.

A second way to price a product or service is what I call "value/benefit relationship." It's very straightforward. What benefit does this product provide and what do people want to pay for it? What is the perceived price that makes sense to people, a price that's not too low and not too high? This is a common-sense way to price, except that you have to do some research. Ask people what they want to pay or call around and see what other people are offering. Notice also that in this approach as well as the first one, the cost to manufacture the product or service isn't taken into account. All that matters is what the customer wants to pay and what other alternatives are available at a similar price in the marketplace.

A third, and completely different approach, is to take the cost to manufacture the product or provide the service, then apply a multiplier or some ratio to double the wholesale cost. This is a common technique because it ensures that the ratio of cost (what you pay for it) to retail (what you sell it for) is in proper balance and set up so the business makes a profit. Although this is one of the most common approaches, it's good to remember the customer doesn't really care what it cost you to make or buy the product or service, so applying a multiple to the cost in order to arrive at the retail may not end up being a good value/benefit relationship.

People sometimes forget this, so they end up with a crazy high price that no one wants to pay or a price that's too low and doesn't take advantage of the market's willingness to pay more.

The last, and fourth, approach to pricing is best used for a totally unique product, one that doesn't exist anywhere else in the marketplace and for which there is no competition. In that case the best pricing technique is "whatever the market will bear." This is typically what you see with rare collectibles or irreplaceable antiques, or for a product that's no longer being made, or perhaps for a drug company that has a unique drug and a monopoly. There's nothing wrong with this approach. It's used by a lot of one-of-a-kind sellers, such as those on eBay. In fact most eBay auctions really are market pricing. An item will sell for the highest price possible, whatever the market will bear. It's a very practical approach.

In the end, I like to look at the four types of pricing models and use a blend of all of them. I like to see us get more market share, I like to see the product have a good value/benefit relationship for the customer, I like to get a normal ratio of cost to retail, and I want to get pretty much whatever the market will bear. Put all these formulas into the discussion, talk about it at work with your associates, and pretty soon a conclusion will become apparent.

Chapter 6

Your Approach to Success

A famous line from Ronald Reagan.

You probably agree that politics is a difficult topic to discuss, and people rarely agree. Ronald Reagan was president of the United States, and we're not going to discuss that, but I really like one of his lines and think of it often. Ronald Reagan said, "I listen to everyone's opinion and then I make up my own mind."

To me that's the best philosophy a leader of a country, or in our case a company, can have. It's so important to listen to everyone's opinion. Not only do we learn more by listening, certainly more than we learn by talking, but we also validate the existence and purpose of the person to whom we are listening. He or she feels so much better because you asked for an opinion.

You may decide to alter your opinion based on what you hear; you may not. The point is that it's important to ask, and you need to encourage everyone to give an honest opinion, not to say yes to you just because you're the boss.

One of my favorite devices in a group is to present a problem, discuss it, lay out some of the arguments on each side of the question, and then go around the table and ask each person to give an opinion. If you really want good opinions you've got to present each side of the argument with enthusiasm and not bias the group. I tell them it doesn't matter, there's no right or wrong answer; I just want to hear some different opinions.

Of course it's important to ask everyone, regardless of where they are in the group hierarchy. Having gotten opinions from everyone, a consensus often begins to emerge and as the leader you may agree with it or not. That's what I liked about the Reagan comment. Listen to everybody, and then make up your own mind.

Believe in yourself and accomplish the impossible.

Do you find that sometimes, or maybe all the time, others meet your ideas with skepticism, or tell you they don't think it can be done? Have you heard reactions like these a lot? I certainly have. It seems thoughout my entire career someone has been telling me that something won't work or isn't likely to succeed.

This reminds me of my favorite fortune I found in a Chinese fortune cookie: "The most satisfying thing in life is doing that which others say you cannot do." Maybe that's why I've had so much fun building a successful business. It's extremely satisfying after others have told you you can't do "it," whatever "it" is. Satisfaction is all the more sweet as a result of overcoming the odds.

On the other hand, let's not overlook one important point. Why do we have trusted friends, advisers and professionals giving us the benefit of their best advice if we're not going to listen to them? And if we do listen, what if our best judgment is to forge ahead?

Let's digress for a moment in the area of sociology. It's been demonstrated in repeated studies that a decision maker, when confronted by a contrary group opinion, is extremely strong in sticking to his or her opinion if just one other person agrees with him or her. If the descision maker loses that one ally, he or she is then statistically much more likely to give up altogether and adopt the group's opinion instead.

For much of my life my father's been that one person to stick with me. I remember so many dark and depressing months and years when it seemed nothing was going to lead to success. Having one person to listen to me and support my ideas made all the difference in the world.

There's the dynamic. You start with an idea and perhaps you get lots of support. More than likely, only one person agrees with you and the rest say it won't work. You really believe in yourself and your idea and no one else does. This last situation is the painful one, the one that will cause you to lose sleep at night. If you turn out to be right in the end, you're a genius.

That's like being Ted Turner and starting CNN (Cable News Network) back when nobody believed that a 24-hour news station could survive. Well, he was right and he proved himself to be a genius.

In the worst case scenario, you try your idea in spite of everyone else, and sure enough it fails, you lose a lot of money. That's a terrible result. And yet, that's what being an entrepreneur is about, making the hard decision to take a chance when no one else thinks it can work, and in the end you make it work.

Here's a thought to help protect against disaster. Unless you are extremely confident about the outcome, don't risk everything you have on your next move. Save something so that if it doesn't work, you can come back and try again.

I remember when my first mail order ad was doing so great for that runner's watch back in 1977. I was spending about a thousand dollars a month on the ad and it was really making money, so eventually I decided to jump to a much bigger magazine, *Popular Science*. The ad cost about $80,000, a huge jump over what I was used to paying, but I'd been doing so well with my ad in *Runner's World* that I figured even if I did just one-fifth as well it would still be at least a break-even. I went ahead with the confidence that the odds were in my favor.

Later, after the magazine ads continued to do well, I decided to try a color catalog. I really didn't know much about what I was doing, but I had a strong hunch that since the products I had placed in magazine ads had performed for me, they would work in a catalog format. I could also add many new products as well. Eventually I mailed out a catalog that cost a lot more money than I had, and it would have bankrupted me if it hadn't performed. Luckily it also did well, and although I didn't make any money on the first mailing, I didn't lose any either.

Then it started to get easier. The obvious strategy was to figure out what products worked, which sold the best, and also which mailing lists did the best. Then all I had to do was follow the guidelines that were now laid out for me in black and white: what products did the customers like, and what groups or lists of people responded to my offerings. That's what I personally love about direct response advertising, in this case the catalog. It immediately gives you the data you need to form new conclusions that will lead you in new and more productive directions.

That's why it seemed natural to me to put The Sharper Image catalog online back in 1995 when the Web was just becoming popular. That was something new to try, and believe me, that idea was met with more skepticism than you can imagine. Lots of people told me it wouldn't work. Trusted associates and even some of my best advisers let me know I was wasting my time. However, I wanted to try it, as I've wanted to try many ideas. Today the Internet is a key part of our business. Other ideas maybe didn't do as well and many haven't survived. That's just the way it is.

No gain without pain.

This is one of my favorite slogans. Someone gave it to me on a paperweight. For many years I really believed it, especially after The Sharper Image went through its painful transition time in 1989/1990. That was the year we had the only financial loss in our history. We had to lay off employees and totally rethink our business strategy with regard to manufacturing our own products. Since that was such a painful period I concluded that the slogan must be right, you cannot achieve gain without pain. I suppose my experience in various exercise programs taught me the same lesson: some pain is unavoidable in order to gain.

I'm not using the paperweight with this slogan anymore. Maybe it's because we've had a number of good years and this year we're having a record year and there isn't any pain at all. In fact, it's been a lot of fun. So where did the pain go that's supposed to be accompanying all this gain? Probably the truth is that there are many years of hard, painful work and then years of easier successes. Let's use the analogy of sailing in the ocean. There are times when the wind is at your back, you're flying easily along, and then there are those times when you're tacking upwind and it's just plain hard, tiring work. I love one of Woody Allen's lines. He said, "Ninety-nine percent of success in life is showing up." It's his humorous way of making the same point and it's so true.

Staying consistently involved and committed for 30 years has been a life passion and a huge effort for me. Of course it's enjoyable and I love it, but it has been a big commitment and I've certainly had difficult times. Not everyone wants to make a long-term, solid, consistent effort. However, if you can make the commitment, I promise you'll see huge results.

Businesses are sometimes built overnight, but more often a business will have a lot more staying power and a lot more quality if it's built slowly, over a long period time. I've also noticed that some years you work harder than ever for very little gain, if any, and in other years success comes easily, probably because of those previous years of slow, painful building.

In summary, don't expect that every time you put in a lot of hard work you'll get an equal amount of success in return. It doesn't work that way. In terms of Pavlovian psychology, you push a lever repeatedly and sometimes, but not every time, you get that little pellet of food. You never know which push of the lever will yield food, but you do know if you keep pushing it, food will eventually fall out. So you keep on pushing. I'm not sure if it's true that there's no gain without pain, but I do know there's no gain without persistence.

God is in the details.

You've heard this before and for good reason. The difference between businesses that succeed and ones that fail is often to be found in the execution of the details. In product design this can mean the way instructions are written, or the way buttons and controls operate, or the way pieces are finished or fit together. In a retail store like The

Sharper Image it's the professionalism of the display, the graphics, the cleanliness of the store, the courtesy of the staff, even our neat and clean dress code. In a service business it might be the consistency of the service, the quality of the presentation, the taste and the freshness of the food.

Whatever the business or endeavor, having a certain obsessive/compulsive attitude toward pulling all the details together is a subtle but powerful message to new customers. Is this a business that has a consistent point of view and execution, or does the inconsistency or sloppiness communicate a message that this is one place the customer might want to avoid?

It doesn't cost more to do things right; in fact, it's usually the opposite. It's often cheaper to do things right the first time because you save the cost of doing it over a second time. In my field of retail we say, "retail is detail." There are a million little details that must be executed correctly. I'm sure that's true in every enterprise.

The next time you're criticized for being overly particular or picky in your approach, don't take it as an insult. It might really be a compliment and it will help you in the long-term. Don't be embarrassed because you want things done a certain way and others seem to have little patience with your exactness and attention to detail.

One of the most detailed and time-consuming efforts for me recently was the introduction of our electric cruiser bike from Sharper Image Design. It's a retro 1940s-look bike that's also electric. It looks great, with blue lights glowing on top of the tank to let you know the status of the charging. When we first introduced it I thought it was being carried in most of our stores. I visited a number of stores and was surprised to find it wasn't there, so I checked with merchandising and learned we hadn't put it in all the stores after all.

I knew it wouldn't sell if our customers couldn't see it, so I made sure we put it in most of the stores. Then while visiting the stores I noticed it was never charged up. The key was never around, the blue lights weren't on, and that meant if a customer wanted to see how it worked, they couldn't. So I started a program to get the bike up on a rear stand so the wheel could turn, made sure we had the key in the tank and that the bike was charged up. That way the customer could twist the throttle and see the rear wheel turning.

A month later I watched customers walk up to the bike; they'd look at it but never twist the throttle to see the wheel turn. Now we have a tag on the handlebar that reads, "Try me. Twist the throttle." It was one detail after another to present this bike properly in all the stores. It was time-consuming and laborious, but it had to be done to make the bike sell. Retail is detail. Your business is, too.

A stylish, coordinated approach inspires confidence.

This is a fun topic. I really love to see businesses that are coordinated— in graphic style, colors, logos, even perhaps a uniform dress code that greets the public. It gives me confidence when a house-painting crew comes out to paint the house and they're wearing matching T-shirts, the graphic design is matched to a van or pickup truck, and all the colors are clean and well presented.

Or when you go into a fast food place, maybe even a locally owned one, and everyone is wearing matching polo shirts or caps or aprons and the tablecloths or placemats all match. It looks professional. There are many examples of coordinated, stylish presentations. Starbucks is one that comes to mind right away. If you visit California, check out In-N-Out Burger. They do a great job at this.

We've made a concerted effort to coordinate all of The Sharper Image. If you visit our stores you'll notice most of them now have our new, updated, black and white interior design. It's a clean, modern look that appeals to men and women alike and shows off our colorful boxes. When you visit you'll also notice the store sales associates coordinate, with black slacks and black polo shirts. And when you go online to www.sharperimage.com you'll see the same black and white theme carried throughout the Website, with colorful product presentations against a neutral background. Even our mail order catalog reflects this theme. The boxes that we design convey the message of coordination of design in all that we do.

That's what it's about. You want to look professional, and that means clean, neat and coordinated. The upfront costs may be a bit higher because you've got to spend a little money on design. But even that can be done inexpensively. You can find it ready-made at many online sites and catalog supply houses. Once you get over the initial expense, it's about the same price to buy supplies that match as it is supplies that don't. Why not do it right? It makes a great first impression and that goes a long way toward getting a customer to return again and again.

Consistency is the hobgoblin of little minds.

That's a funny phrase, isn't it? Consistency is the hobgoblin of little minds. This means that it's important to be willing to change your mind and to have those you work with understand why it's okay. You have to realize that most people don't like a change of direction.

If you've previously made a decision and everyone has supported you and your leadership, they aren't going to be happy when you change direction. I try to tell people I never change my mind until I have new information. Doesn't that make sense?

If you've heard a new or better opinion, or learned some new information, why wouldn't you want to make the best decision possible based on the latest facts? It's your responsibility to do exactly that and then to sell these changes to your organization.

Of course it helps if you acknowledge the incredible effort everyone has already put in and apologize for asking them to shift direction. This shows them the respect you feel for their work. That's what they want to hear. Now you've gotten them lined up to shift direction to the new and better course and every factor is optimized for success. You've incorporated the newest and best information into your strategy, you've smoothed over the ruffled feathers of those who were inconvenienced and the whole group is now moving toward a new and better goal.

To me there's nothing more important than staying flexible, being ready to change your mind as soon as you learn something new. Life is so challenging that if you're not prepared to turn on a dime, it's hard to make the best decision and then move forward.

Chapter 7

Making Sure You Succeed

Fail your way to success.

We've already talked about this, but it's so important. I want to talk about taking action. I'm a firm believer that the most important thing you can do to get moving in a positive direction is to take action as soon as possible. Do something. There's always the risk you may make a mistake in choosing a particular path and the sooner you find out you're wrong the better off you are.

Your life is not supposed to resemble a civil service job where you spend your entire working life. Rather, you need to get on the right course as quickly as you can. I refer to this process as failing your way to success. You try different approaches and techniques, and sooner or later you find something that works for you.

During the first 20 years of The Shaper Image I tried so many things that didn't work and so many things that did. I'm the best example of someone who failed his way to success.

Plan for the worst case.

It's often been said that a good planning tool is to think ahead to what you'll do if the worst-case scenario comes true. Obviously that's a pretty scary thought, but it does give you a good sense of how to mentally prepare. Realistically it's unlikely the worst case will occur, it practically never does, but you'll sleep better if you've already thought it through.

What are you going to do if that unfortunate moment does occur? Think about how you will recover, how you will finance your next effort, how you will make up the lost sales, the lost investment or the lost effort. But don't worry; this is a fail-safe disaster planning tool. Most of your efforts will never result in a worst-case scenario. If you're prepared, you won't be caught off guard.

No surprises.

A paperweight sat on my desk for many years. It had this simple slogan engraved on it, "No surprises." I guess it was my subtle way of sending a message to everyone who came in to meet with me. It was pretty clear. It's much easier to manage a business on a day to day basis when there are no major surprises. Now that The Sharper Image is a public stock company you can bet an unpleasant surprise is the last thing any fund manager or shareholder wants to hear about.

When I'm meeting with my executive managers or with an associate on the sales floor in a store, the last thing I want to learn from the conversation is some new, unknown, unpleasant surprise. The surprise might be that some budget item was way out of line, or some product was hopelessly late being delivered, or that the quality was so poor we might have to stop selling it. These types of major surprises are quite disconcerting and can negatively impact sales planning, especially around critical selling times like the holidays.

Over the years, I've seen a change in the way our business reacts to surprises. When the business was smaller, surprises felt like earthshaking threats. Sometimes it was learning that a key executive was resigning for a better career opportunity. That often happens with smaller start-up companies because talented people often don't have the patience to wait for a small company to grow up. It's human nature, but it's still jarring when it happens.

Start-ups and small companies also have less financial resiliency, so any event with financial consequences can drastically affect the ability of the business to provide adequate cash flow, meet the payroll, pay the checks on time and so on. As The Sharper Image grew and matured, surprises like these were less impactful. Today, each surprise has a smaller impact on the overall business and they're not so vitally important.

I've finally taken the paperweight off my desk. There will always be surprises, but it's nice to look forward to the time when your business has been around long enough, has enough financial staying power, and a strong enough brand name, that you can have confidence your business is going to survive the inevitable surprises. Until that moment, keep thinking, "no surprises."

Momentum takes on a life of its own.

Whether there is positive momentum in your business or negative momentum, it does seem to be true that once the momentum builds a head of steam, it takes on a life of its own. When we had our unbroken run of successes from 1977 to 1987 the impressive sales expansion covered up a multitude of small mistakes, and the growth continued. It was great.

When we ran into problems in 1989, the momentum turned negative and it took years to turn it around. This is similar to what happens with the U.S. economy. When there's a strong expansion it seems like it's never going to end, and when the economy is spiraling down month after month, people get discouraged and wonder if it will ever turn up again.

Knowing these facts, how can we take advantage of it in our own businesses? A positive expansionary period is the time to expand advertising, spend money to acquire customers, increase prospecting, and perhaps try some wild and crazy marketing effort that normally might be a little bit of a stretch. Conversely, when living through a tough period when things are contracting, cut all those frivolous or uncertain marketing efforts. Now's the time to tighten your belt and try to get through, and don't forget to do everything you can to keep morale up during the difficult times.

When The Sharper Image suffered a poor financial momentum and bad press in 1990, we actually put posters up around the company with this message, "Perception lags reality." I constantly told our associates that things were going to get better, and in fact that process had already been put in place. Nevertheless, positive results on the bottom line weren't apparent, and I felt it was important to reassure them that we were doing better, even if it hadn't shown up yet in earnings or sales.

In other words, perception lags reality. We got through that difficult period and entered our best period, and in your business you'll see the same thing happen. Don't let the downturns get you down. Instead, start working toward that positive momentum.

Have confidence, even when you're losing sleep at night.

During the most difficult times when the very viability and future of your business is unsure, there's a strong temptation for some people to jump ship. It's just human nature. Some of your closest associates will stick with you because they love the company, respect you, or genuinely believe that your leadership can turn things around. Others will stay because they don't have a better place to go, and as long as they're collecting their salary, simple inertia will keep them in place.

Others, especially those who have little stomach for stress and uncertainty, or those who see themselves on a fast track to success, will start looking for greener pastures. This can be extremely stressful during a critical period when you're already suffering from worry and frayed nerves. It can be a serious blow to your business to lose a critical position at a time when you can least afford it. It's one of the most precarious moments in the life of your business.

What to do? One obvious step is to add stock option grants or end-of-year bonuses that are guaranteed, but only for those who stick around to collect them. Be honest with your people. Tell them it's a critical time. You really need them and want them to stay, and to reward them for staying you'll offer extra compensation to be paid 12 or 24 months down the road. Now they have an incentive to stay. And please, keep your demeanor upbeat and positive. Never demonstrate a lack of confidence or display a shred of self-doubt.

There's a famous scene in the movie *Funny Girl* with Barbra Streisand and Omar Sharif. He plays a world class gambler, Nicky, and the lesson he delivers is that whether he's winning or losing, he must always appear to be confident and in control. That's pretty good advice. We all want to be seen as real human beings, but the fact is that you, as a leader, must convey confidence.

A near brush with bankruptcy (subtitled: what hours should you work?)

Clearly, when you're working for someone else it's great to show up at the office early and leave late. It makes a good impression. If it's your own business it's a different story. For many years I made it a point to be the first one at the office and the last one to leave. I followed the old adage that the boss should be the first to arrive and the last to go home.

The Sharper Image had a terribly difficult year in 1989/1990. It was the first year in our history we experienced a financial loss. We deserved it, by the way. We had become inefficient and wasteful with money and we were too casual about controlling the expenses.

We'd had about 15 successful years in a row, so we were not prepared to cope with adversity. We were soft and spoiled, I think. Success had come so easily to us, we didn't develop the discipline that we needed.

Here we were in a terrible recession that began in 1989 and continued into 1990 and things were tough. As a management team, however, it was a constructive experience. I thought hard about how we had gotten where we were, and what we were doing wrong during this wasteful, financially difficult year.

As it turned out, we survived. We learned to cope with adversity and we became much better managers. There were layoffs, the first layoffs in our history, and we completely restrategized our merchandising. It was a painful period but we came out a better company for it. From that point on we continued to do better and better. In fact we're having the best year in our history, both in revenues and earnings. It would never have happened except for the fact that we got through the difficult years and learned some new disciplines.

One of our board members said something to me during that difficult year that really inspired me. He said, "You know, Richard, getting to this point took really good merchandising and that was easy for you. Now you're going to prove to be a good business manager as well." When he said that I realized, now's the time to prove to myself that I can manage this problem. Maybe I was lucky, maybe I was smart (probably lucky), but fortunately I got through.

However, I did think about how I wanted to spend my time every day in a way that was most likely to help us survive. I realized that coming in first in the morning and leaving last at night was not necessarily the way I worked the best. Sometimes my best thinking is done walking in the morning, or daydreaming at home on my computer, or talking to people on the telephone.

At that time I thought The Sharper Image might end up in bankruptcy court. We didn't of course, but I thought we might. And I saw myself standing before the judge and I'd tell him, "Your Honor, I know the facts show that my business is bankrupt, but please be lenient with me because, you see, I showed up early every single day." And I realized how silly that would sound. I concluded that you have to do the best thing you can for the success of your business, even if the best thing is not coming to work at eight o'clock in the morning. The very best thing I can do for my business is to make sure it does well so that everyone who works there will have a future with us.

That's how I arrived at my present approach to hours in the office. I come in as often as necessary and I don't feel guilty. Many days I work at home in the morning and head to the office at ten or eleven. Some days I work on my computer at home. Of course it helps that I have a terrific right-hand person to run the day-to-day operation and supervise all the different aspects of our business. Our entire management team is solid and accomplished. Obviously that makes a huge difference, but it's taken me a long time to get comfortable with this approach. It works for me, and thank goodness I didn't have to tell that to a judge in bankruptcy court!

Chapter 8

Solving Problems

How to resolve legal disputes faster and less expensively.

Over the years we've had several legal disputes between The Sharper Image and other parties. These come up for a wide variety of reasons. Sometimes we're wrong; sometimes the other party's wrong. (Actually I think most of the time the other party was wrong!) Sometimes the initiation of communication by our attorney began a series of expensive and combative interactions that culminated years later in a settlement. Both parties walked away poorer in time and money for the experience.

There were instances when, if I had picked up the phone personally and gotten involved, we could have solved the problem right away with minimal expense and aggravation. This is because many such disputes are business problems as much as legal problems, and sometimes having a business discussion is a lot more to the point than letting the attorneys take over.

Attorneys do have a tendency to let things drag on. I hate to sound jaded, but let's face facts. There are those attorneys who, with all good intentions, let the hours roll along, collect their billings and pat themselves on the back for doing a conscientious job for the client. That's just the way it is.

One unfortunate but true story sticks in my mind. At the time of the Southern California earthquake in 1994 we had a Sharper Image store in Sherman Oaks, California, near Los Angeles. The store was badly damaged in the earthquake and our attorney felt we were legally correct in closing the store and walking away from the lease owing nothing. He thought that was a clause in the contract. Our chief operating officer was handling the case for me and working with our attorney. The attorney was sure of his position, advising us all along and I was letting them handle it.

Time passed, the case eventually went to trial and we lost. We had attorney's fees and damages of more than half a million dollars. The amazing fact is that several years later I happened to meet the owner of the Sherman Oaks building. He was a very nice man who loved The Sharper Image. He said he had really appreciated being our landlord and that he loved our products and our stores. Then he told me if I had just called him personally when the incident occurred we probably could have settled the entire matter on our own without any attorney involvement. It would have cost me less than a $100,000. What a lesson!

That was a big mistake on my part and one that I'm never going to make again. Hopefully you'll learn from it, too. Don't be afraid to pick up the phone and try to solve a legal dispute, especially if it's really a business problem more than a legal one, and most of them are.

Paying bills on time, or "the check's in the mail."

People develop reputations over time, and businesses do, too. Part of the reputation that will stick with you for your entire business career is your credit history. Specifically, how you pay your bills. I've always been amazed how some businesses, especially the larger ones, take advantage of their smaller vendors by dragging out the payments on open invoices, essentially paying their bills late. Obviously it isn't ethical.

If you provide a product or service and the terms are on credit and the due date is clearly specified, there's really no excuse, other than a legal disagreement, not to pay the money on the date specified. Anything later than that and you're taking advantage of the seller. It's like cheating. You might get away with it one or more times, but it's still cheating; actually more like stealing.

Let's not forget that when you pay your bills late you're also setting yourself up to receive poor treatment from the vendor. Why should they give you their full attention when you're their worst paying account? I'd rather be their best paying account, and know they'll give me great follow-through. Additionally, if you ever need to ask them for something like extended terms to help you through a lean period, you know they're going to be more receptive and trusting if you've always paid them on time. And don't overlook the opportunity to pay early and get an additional discount. It's expected that if you're paying in 10 or 20 days you can ask for a discount off the invoice price.

When I first started my office supply business I was delivering office products in the morning, selling in the afternoon, and typing up bills at night on the kitchen table. I'd write, "Net 30 days" on the invoices. I actually expected the check would be there by the 31st day. I was so surprised when the checks didn't show up by then. So I'd pick up the phone and call these people and say, "Gee whiz, what happened?" I think my naiveté and my candor caught these people off guard, because then they'd actually send me the check.

I learned you've got to personally follow up and nag people. It's amazing how the biggest businesses, the ones with the most money, are sometimes (not always, but sometimes) the worst at paying their bills, but you have to insist on it, tell them what you expect, be demanding in a polite way. And as far as paying bills, all my life I've made it a point to always pay bills on time or sooner. People appreciate it so much and it adds to your reputation.

My vacations always turn into focus groups.

I'm a great believer in the value of vacations, even though I admit I don't take more than anyone else. Vacations provide some of the best thinking time for entrepreneurs. You can see your business more clearly when you're a little bit farther away from it. I've had some really good ideas or input from others while on vacation.

I used to go to a particular spa resort where there was a fairly high percentage of women. This was during the time that The Sharper Image was more of a man's store than a woman's store. I'd often ask the women at the spa what they thought about my stores, and it was interesting how consistent their criticism and feedback was. They kept telling me the stores were too technical, too cold, too gray and really not that appealing to women in terms of ambience.

After that I set plans in motion for a whole new architecture for our stores. Today most of The Sharper Image stores have been remodeled to our new look — a clean, crisp black and white look. Both men and women have commented enthusiastically on how well it works, how it appeals to everyone. I'm convinced the redesign enabled us to attract a new group of female customers that we would never have appealed to with the old look. Today our customer base reflects about half men and half women.

You might wonder how many people need to be asked before you can count on the validity of their opinions. How statistically reliable is it when you're doing focus groups of just two, three, five, 10 people? Again and again in my experience I find that if I ask 10 people the same question, a reasonably clear trend emerges after the tenth answer. That isn't very many people, is it? Yet it works as a valuable predictor even with such a small sample.

Try it with a problem you can't quite resolve. Ask 10 people — they could be in the business or they could be friends or even strangers — and you'll see a clear answer sooner than you think. Once in awhile you may get a split decision, but that tells you something in itself. The Sharper Image doesn't use focus groups because it's so easy to ask people for their opinion, and a trend usually becomes quite apparent.

Listen to your customers. I've spent many hours in our stores talking to customers and asking them what they think. I ask them to tell me something they like about our business and something they don't like. They're a ready source of tips on ways to improve your business. I enjoy personally asking these questions and personally hearing the responses, and we save a lot of money on focus groups.

Try a mini-vacation this morning.

One of my favorite things is to vary each week's routine so I don't get into a repetitive rut. I may take off a morning or an afternoon, and once in a great while even take the whole day off. But I don't really take it off. Sometimes I work at home via phone and e-mail, and sometimes I drive somewhere and make cell phone calls along the way.

By changing your location or staying out of the office you do get a break, which feels good, like a mini-vacation. This is especially important for the owner of a business because you can't easily take real vacations, and because you need to be there in person to supervise others.

That's why the mini-vacation works so well. You avoid getting burned out because you're taking small breaks during the week. You definitely don't want to get into such a rut that you do get burned out. That won't help your business grow.

Another thing to remember is that growing your business is like a marathon, not a sprint. There may be times when you feel like you're sprinting, but in general you'll want to pace yourself so you always feel good and relaxed. Sprinting will just burn you out and then you'll crash. Not good. You may have noticed that when your stress level is slightly higher than what you can tolerate, you don't feel productive. At least that's the way I am.

When the stress level is just slightly below what I can easily accommodate, I feel fine. In other words, try to keep your workload slightly below the stress level at which you start feeling uncomfortable and out of control.

Think of life like a marathon. You know a marathon's a 26-mile run, and ideally you want to start at a comfortable pace and speed up throughout the race. You don't want to start at a sprint and then fall off and limp in. You actually want to pace yourself. Your life and your career should be run the same way. A mini-vacation is designed to keep you fresh and energized. As you go through life and as your business grows, you want to maintain a steady pace and you want to speed up; you don't want to burn out.

Work, career, marriage and family.

Many marriages break up over one spouse's dedication, or maybe over-dedication, to work. Haven't we all heard stories of people whose marriages have ended because one partner was too preoccupied with work? This is where the concept of the mini-vacation comes to the forefront. Try to take time now and then to do small things with your spouse. Maybe have lunch together, or breakfast, or an afternoon spa trip for his and her massages. A little goes a long way. And don't, under any circumstances, forget anniversaries, birthdays and other important dates that let the other person know they're on your mind. This is meaningful stuff.

While we're on the subject, let's add family and children to this mix. I'm a total believer in the value of family. I believe in being home for dinner, families sitting down together for meals, or going to sporting events. All the wonderful things that make family life great. And when it comes to choosing between survival of family relationships and love for your children, or working overtime to build your career, I say the family comes first. Of course that's just me; you may feel differently.

There's the story about the person who, after a lifetime of hard work, finally reaches his deathbed. He reflects on his entire life and says, "Oh, I wish I had spent more time at the office." Is this likely? I don't think so! The moral of the story is that we're only here for a limited time and there are many worthwhile things to do. Certainly work is one of them, but let's not spend so much time working that we neglect time with our family or time for ourselves. Too many people look back and say they wish they had spent more time with their kids or family.

There's more than one way to skin a cat.

There are so many ways to reach a goal. Sometimes we get frustrated because we're fixated on reaching it a certain way and nothing works. It occasionally happens in our Sharper Image Design product engineering group. We may have a minor mechanical engineering problem and we'll keep working and working on it, and before long the entire project is stalled because of that one stumbling block. Here's where you need to think outside the box to brainstorm creative ways to solve a problem using a totally different approach.

Never think that the path you set out on is the only one that will lead to the finish. Remember to give your associates permission to take a fresh approach, even a radically different one, in order to solve a problem.

A slightly different way to solve a problem is to simply drop the issue altogether. If you're trying to add a certain feature to a product and it's not working, why not drop the feature altogether? That's an easy solution. It's come up many times for me at work.

We encountered a problem with our Sharper Image-designed, best-selling eyeglass cleaning product. You put your eyeglasses in the tank and it automatically cleans them.

But here's the problem: After the eyeglasses are cleaned, how do we get the liquid solution off the lenses without leaving any spots? This is similar to a dishwasher problem. You put your glassware in the dishwasher and when they've dried you don't want to see any spots on them. But a dishwasher uses tremendous heat. Our product is battery-operated, sits on a countertop, and there's no heat. We couldn't seem to eliminate those little spots.

We spent about five years trying to solve this maddening problem. Finally, it just got so frustrating that it occurred to me to take a different approach altogether. We finally came up with a secret silicone additive to the cleaning solution. The silicone actually fills in microscopic scratches on the lenses.

Now when the cycle's finished and the machine opens up and presents the eyeglasses, the customer quickly and easily polishes the lenses with the included microfiber cloth. The lenses are totally conditioned, as good as new, and look fantastic with that very slight polishing. In other words, the slight negative of having the customer polish the lenses at the end of the cycle has been turned into a positive, because now the special solution actually improves the quality of the lenses. Not only does the automatic eyeglass cleaner do a good job of cleaning, but the microscopic scratches are magically filled in and the eyeglasses are better than ever.

The technique of thinking outside the box is probably one that's learned over time. You need to step back from the problem, ask for a fresh approach, give others permission to try something completely different, and eventually you'll find a new path. It's like turning lemons into lemonade.

Chapter 9

Some Final Thoughts

May we please talk about manners?

You might wonder why I'm throwing this in. Here's why: I have a strong belief that manners make a difference, in the long-term success or failure of your business, and it costs nothing. Your business will make a great impression using good manners and politeness when encountering customers. Start with the magic words like "please" or "thank you," and "yes ma'am" and "yes sir." These are absolutely guaranteed to win friends and customer loyalty.

A small but important conversational device is to remember to use the words "yes" or "yes sir" instead of the slang, "uh-huh" or "okay" when speaking to a customer. Imagine a customer calls to ask if you have a certain item in stock. The sales rep says, "Yes sir, we have both colors in stock. Would you like me to hold one for you?" Now compare that with "Yeah, we've got some," or even worse, "Uh-huh." That may be fine for teenagers working in a clothing chain, but not for a national business for grownups. Which sounds better to you?

The nice thing about good manners is that the customers who appreciate it will really appreciate it, and the ones who don't notice won't mind at all if good manners are used. Thank you!

Management by opportunity.

If there's one guiding principle that might describe my management style, it's management by opportunity. What that means to me is that business, like life, is fluid and always changing. Opportunities arise and disappear, obstacles pop up, new problems arise, and new solutions become apparent. Your job is to think creatively and stay flexible. You will inevitably go down paths that turn out to be dead ends. In fact, I would even go so far as to say that you have to try a lot of different things and many won't work. That's just the way it is, and you can't let it discourage you.

It might sound funny to say this, but I really believe that often you must fail your way to success. The person who's afraid to try never has the opportunity to fail, and also never has the opportunity to succeed. The successful entrepreneur keeps trying, looking for the next opportunity to succeed.

Over the years I've tried a lot of different ideas and many of them didn't work. There was a Sharper Image

Health catalog, there was a Sharper Image Spa catalog, there were Sharper Image Spa stores. There was a Sharper Image wine club, and even a Sharper Image home collection catalog that sold furniture. None of these concepts are alive and kicking today.

On the other hand, the craziest idea I ever had was to begin manufacturing our own proprietary products. That was easily the one idea most likely to fail, most likely to bring down the whole company, and had very remote odds of succeeding. Yet it not only succeeded, it's one of the main reasons that The Sharper Image is surviving and prospering today.

Sometimes in life a wave comes along, and you hope you have the instincts and the judgment to know when to get up on that wave and ride it in. Some people might call it luck. I prefer to think that luck is really preparation meeting opportunity. If you're prepared and you've done your homework, you'll be able to take advantage of the opportunity when it presents itself to you. That's how you'll climb on top of the wave and ride it all the way in, and others will say, "Wow, weren't you lucky?" And you'll think, No, I was prepared and I took advantage of the opportunity.

Good things come to those who wait.

A long time ago I met Arthur Jones, the inventor of Nautilus Gym Equipment. You've probably seen or used their machines at one time or another. The Sharper Image introduced the first Nautilus machines for the home. Arthur called — I didn't know the man at the time — but he called to say how much he respected us and felt we were the best place to launch his new line of smaller home machines, especially the first abdominal or waist–trimming Nautilus machine.

Arthur invited me to visit him at his home in Jumbolair, Florida. It had a 10,000-foot landing strip for his two jets, a Boeing 707 and a Cessna Citation. His original business had actually been selling wild animals to zoos. I'm not sure that's a good idea, but that's what he did. The 707 was used to fly back and forth to Africa, bringing back elephants, alligators, monkeys and other wild animals to populate his zoo at Jumbolair.

Arthur was an unusual person who had accomplished a lot, and he was brilliant to have invented the Nautilus machines. He was absolutely right that people would buy a reasonably priced machine for home use, especially if it was designed to reduce the stomach bulge. It probably helped promote the product that it was modeled in our catalog by Terry Jones, the former Miss Florida beauty who was Arthur's fourth wife. She was athletic and beautiful and the photography was very well done. We introduced the Nautilus home abdominal machine on the cover of our Sharper Image catalog and it sold better than we could have ever imagined. We sold thousands and thousands of them.

Arthur said one thing that sticks with me even today. He said most people create something, or build a business, and then cash out too early. They don't realize they can maximize results by sticking with it for the long term. He said most people think short term, and that's a mistake. I realize this truism was not proven true during the explosion, or implosion, of the "dot-com stock" bubble. In that case the ones that cashed out quickly made the most money; however, that wasn't really a business, it was a bubble in the stock market.

When you're building your business, or your career with a company, there's a lot to be said for sticking around long enough to see it bear fruit. It doesn't always happen right away, but eventually you'll be rewarded. Certainly for me at The Sharper Image, after almost 30 years, it's really begun to pay off. It's been a long road, and it's gotten better over time.

Good things come to those who are impatient.

If there's one description that applies to me it's that I'm always in a hurry to get started, to take the first step. We've discussed the fact that if all objections must be overcome nothing will ever be accomplished. Along the same line, the more impatient you are, the sooner you're going to get what you want. There's a delicate balance between being seen as pushy or rude, and being politely impatient. I like being polite, but I'm also impatient. I'm the kind of person who, when waiting in line at a cashier's station, isn't too bashful to ask, "Isn't there someone else here who can ring up sales?" I know patience is a virtue; I also know that impatience often gets you what you want. Each plays an important role in your business life and your personal life as well. You need a healthy balance, but don't be reluctant to be impatient now and then.

I'll never forget when I first moved to San Francisco and started my office supply business. I'd go to the financial district, I'd knock on doors, I'd walk the sidewalks, and I kept thinking, People, get out of my way. I'm in a hurry to get to my next appointment. I'm in a hurry to get somewhere. I was literally impatient simply walking down the sidewalk.

I can't count the number of meetings I've attended in my life to look at sales results. Perhaps we mailed out a mail order or a catalog or a promotion and we saw great results on a limited scale. I'm impatient to mail out five times the number. Everybody else is thinking, Shouldn't we go more slowly? and I'm thinking, Why? We've got these great results, let's get going. That's just the way I am. That sense of urgency to get moving once you see a course of action laid out before you is so important. I guess you could say good things come to those who do not wait.

Tomorrow is the beginning.

You're an optimist; you're an entrepreneur. You know some of these ideas make a lot of sense. You've got the ambition and the desire to make your business or your career more successful than it is. Why not? It's not that hard, but you have to be diligent, persistent. You've got to take that first step; you've got to begin to think where you want to be in five years or 10 years, and what steps will take you there.

You begin to think about that first step, and before you know it a day has gone by and you haven't done anything. This is perfectly normal. Break it down into a smaller steps and keep asking yourself which small step can you actually accomplish? Once you take that first small step you'll feel so good about yourself.

Now you're ready for step two. You march on every day, moving forward, and before you know it a year has gone by and you're excited because you've accomplished a lot more than you ever imagined you would. You're on the road to really building something.

Many times you're going to find you've got to take one step back before you can take two steps forward. There will be many discouraging moments as well as many wonderful moments of elation. That's what's so great about being an entrepreneur and doing your own thing. Gosh, it's frustrating, and gosh, it's so elevating. So don't get discouraged, have a lot of confidence in yourself, and I know you'll have terrific results.

I've enjoyed creating this book, and I hope it's helped you. Good luck, and I wish you every success.